Live a Life of
Significance

Senske, Kurt Martin, 1959-

The Calling : live a life of significance / Kurt Senske.
    p. cm.

 Includes bibliographical references (p.   ).

 ISBN 978-0-7586-1666-1

 1. Vocation--Lutheran Church. 2. Lutheran Church--Doctrines. I. Title.
 BV4740.S46 2010

 248.4'841--dc22
               2010018342

3 4 5 6 7 8 9 10 11 12   ·   20 19 18 17 16 15 14 13 12 11

Kurt Senske

The Calling

Live a Life of Significance

CONCORDIA PUBLISHING HOUSE • SAINT LOUIS

This book is dedicated to my wife, Laurie,

my daughter, Sydney,

and to my parents, Al and Ruth Senske.

Collectively, they have modeled for
me how to live a life of significance.

Contents

PART ONE

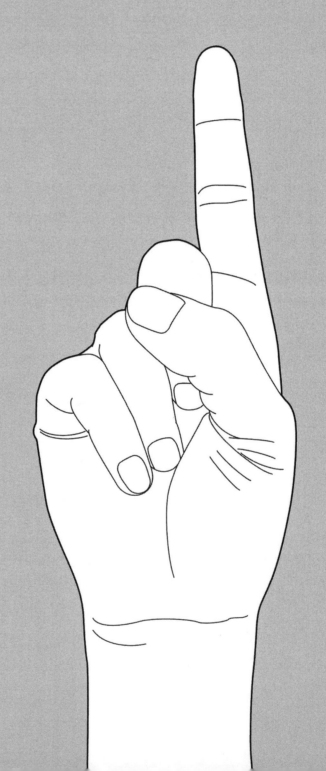

What Is Significance?

For You formed my inward parts;
You knitted me together in my mother's womb.
—Psalm 139:13

To live a life of significance is, above all, a spiritual undertaking. In this undertaking, we can employ certain strategies of our twenty-first-century world, integrating biblical wisdom with secular research to optimize our unique gifts from God. In the process, our days are transformed from the drudgery of repetition, frustration, and heartbreak, to lives marked by integrity and intention. Our lives, if they are to be truly significant, must flow from our Christian faith. What, exactly, does this mean? The following are truths of our faith that cannot be compromised:

- Jesus Christ died and rose for the forgiveness of our sins, and we are saved by His grace alone.

- We are brought to the beginning of each day forgiven of our past sins and freed to be of service to God and His people.

- We are gathered into the community of faith, the Church, where we hear Christ's Word and partake of His holy meal.

Although God is the agent of transformation in our lives, we are not left without responsibility. By these means, these truths of faith mentioned above, the Holy Spirit enables us to live the life God created uniquely for us. Through these means, the Spirit empowers us to multiply our talents through our callings to family, professional, community, and congregational lives, thus giving Him the glory. This is what it means to live a life of significance. Just how effective we are in our quest is ultimately a matter of God's grace for us. Our chances are greatly increased when we walk hand in hand with God, use the resources at our disposal, ask for forgiveness when we stumble, and boldly step forward.

Let the Christ-help journey begin.

Christ-Help, Not Self-Help

The heart of man plans his way,
but the LORD establishes his steps. —**Proverbs 16:9**

How does God want me to live out the rest of my life? More accurately, how have I been called to participate in God's life? If you are like me, questions such as these continue. How do I discern God's plan for me? How might I multiply the talents God has entrusted to me in my family, work, community, and church roles? Sometimes the questions become less esoteric and more immediate. How do I pay the bills at the end of the month? How do I find a job that motivates and inspires? What should I major in at college? Why is my family life in such a shambles? How do I live a life of meaning and significance?

Belatedly, the realization hits us: perhaps we are not living the life God has created uniquely for us.

Ten years ago I embarked—obsessively, some would say—on a quest to understand what it means to live a life of significance. My goal was to create a road map. However, in the process, I discovered one already existed. Nevertheless, I read voraciously, pondered pertinent Bible passages, wrote two books that touch on the topic, and talked to hundreds of people. Two questions consistently surfaced: (1) How do I distinguish between God's will and my own self-interest, and are they ever the same? (2) If I perceived His will correctly, would I have the courage to pursue it wholeheartedly? This book is not just another in a market overrun with self-help literature. A quick scan of titles in the local bookstore shows there is no shortage of these, from both secular and Christian perspectives. Many are destined to disappoint, but not because they are poorly written or lack good ideas. These self-help books fall short for a number of reasons, not the least of which is the author's promise of a quick fix or path to success. The books are designed to help us help ourselves to get what *we* want, and assume that attaining our goals is equivalent to having a life of significance. The fact is that even if we do achieve some level of success, we still come no closer to knowing whether we are living the life that God has created uniquely for us. Being "successful" and living the life that God intended are not necessarily the same.

Being 'successful' and living the life that God intended are not necessarily the same.

The good news is that, as Christians, we don't need to rely on the self-help gurus to discover meaning in our lives. In Baptism God gave us self-worth. Thus, in a world that measures worth by material goods, we are already ahead; we approach the starting line secure in the knowledge that God's action *for us* through Jesus Christ infuses our life with meaning. This truth turns our quest on its head from self-help to a Christ-help perspective. This change makes all the difference.

Much self-help literature is ineffective because it fails to acknowledge the dual nature of humankind. Martin Luther's description of us as *simul justus et peccator*—at the same time saint and sinner—is the classic expression of our human condition. We are sinful *and* redeemed. The Greek philosopher Plato, in his epic work *The Republic*, describes the human plight as a charioteer trying to control two strong horses, each wanting to head in a different direction. Not only are we unable to measure up to God's will for us, there are times we don't even want to. In our more honest moments, we can relate all too well with St. Augustine, who asked God to make him pure, but not yet!

It is virtually impossible for us to live up to the secular standard of success. The quest for enough beauty, power, wealth, or toys is doomed to fail because it depends on our efforts. It is by this very recognition that we, as Christians, begin our quest with humility, acknowledging God's forgiveness for us, overwhelmed by grace. We grasp the biblical truth that, whatever goal we pursue, we succeed because "we walk by faith, not by sight" (2 Corinthians 5:7). The Holy Spirit empowers us to stand in this world with confidence, like David did in the presence of mighty Goliath, and come out victorious. The promise of eternal life with God refocuses our vision and energy to meet the needs of those we encounter today—family, neighbors, colleagues, and clients. We look for and reach out in service to the sick, abused, imprisoned, and others who make up "the least of these."

2

CHRIST CALLS US TO PLAY ON HIS TEAM

But You, O Lord, are a God merciful and gracious,
slow to anger and abounding in steadfast love
and faithfulness. —**Psalm 86:15**

God seeks to claim us as one of His own. We do not find God; God finds us. Through the death and resurrection of Jesus, God has broken down the wall of sin that separates us from Him, and He makes our union with Him a reality. We call this gift grace. "For by grace you have been saved through faith. And this is not your own doing; it is the gift of God, not a result of works, so that no one may boast" (Ephesians 2:8–9).

Through Baptism God claims us as members of His family—His team, to use a sports analogy. His call doesn't allow compromise. Like Peter and the rest of the twelve apostles, who at times tried defining discipleship on their terms, we sometimes try to renegotiate terms of what our participation on the team will look like: "I will play for You most Sundays, God, but I won't be able to play for You at work." Or, "I will be ready to play *after* I get married." Or, "Once I make my first million, I'll be better positioned." Or, "Let me enjoy my time in college, then I'll settle down and get serious about playing for You." However, Jesus demands that we follow Him without wavering:

> No one can serve two masters, for either he will hate the
> one and love the other, or he will be devoted to the one
> and despise the other. You cannot serve God and money.
> (Matthew 6:24)

Jesus reminds us that "Not everyone who says to Me, 'Lord, Lord,' will enter the kingdom of heaven, but the one who does the will of My Father who is in heaven" (Matthew 7:21). Dietrich Bonhoeffer accurately states that when we respond to God's call, we intentionally separate ourselves from our previous existence in order to create our new life.[1] Simply put, it is impossible for us to live the life that God created uniquely for us *and* continue to live in our old ways.

Simply put, it is impossible for us to live
the life that God created uniquely for us
and continue to live in our old ways.

Through faith we have been called to be children of God. Through Baptism we have been born anew—given a new heart, a new life. We are set on a path walked by Jesus, who "is the way and the truth and the life" (John 14:6). Apart from Him we can do nothing (John 15:5). Jesus came to give life to the full (John

10:10). We rejoice in His promise, "I am the resurrection and the life. Whoever believes in Me, though he die, yet shall he live" (John 11:25). Paul sums up the charter of God's covenant with us in what are among the most reassuring and uncompromising words of Scripture: "We were buried therefore with Him by baptism into death, in order that, just as Christ was raised from the dead by the glory of the Father, we too might walk in newness of life" (Romans 6:4).

Yet, even in the face of such overwhelming encouragement, we find living a Christ-filled life difficult. It would seem that a beat up and dated leather-bound Bible and a 500-year-old catechism are simply no match for the overwhelming combination of today's skewed values and unrelenting peer pressure. These delude us into believing that happiness is just one purchase or pay raise away. We become enslaved to our ego. We have all experienced the consequences of our futile resistance to God's call, the missed opportunities, heartache, and turmoil that come at the expense of our refusal to allow God to be at the center of our lives. When the Spirit finally breaks down our wall of hesitation, and we realize what we have been denying ourselves, we are made ready to choose a new way. The question is "How?" What strategies can we incorporate to live the life that God created uniquely for us as His saved children?

3

THE CALL

And as He passed by, He saw Levi the son
of Alphaeus sitting at the tax booth, and He said to
him, "Follow Me." And he rose and followed Him.
—Mark 2:14

We often talk about finding our "calling," our "vocation." Both terms are derived from the Latin *vocare*, or *voice*, and its Greek equivalent, *kalein*, to *call*. As Christians, we believe that God calls us, one by one, to serve Him through our worship and service to our neighbor.

The secular world sometimes co-opts the word *vocation* for its own purposes, using it to describe our professional occupation only. However, as Christians, the words *vocation* and *calling* (which I use interchangeably) have a much broader meaning. You and I are called to serve God well in every distinct legitimate realm of our lives—family, profession, community, and congregation. Each distinct yet overlapping calling demands that we develop and use our God-given gifts and talents as we daily serve all those with whom we come into contact.

Martin Luther used the analogy of wearing "masks of God" when by our service we carry out our various roles. A father, for example, wears the mask of God when he coaches his daughter's soccer team. Likewise, the firefighter wears the mask of God when he puts out the fire at the house down the street. My wife, Laurie, wears the mask of God when she delivers *Meals on Wheels* to her assigned clients. My daughter, Sydney, wears the mask of God when she babysits the children next door. I wear the mask of God in a number of roles, including spouse, father, son, son-in-law, brother, brother-in-law, uncle, pet owner, boss, employee, mentor, author, congregation member, speaker, consultant, board member, donor, volunteer, friend, neighbor, and political advocate. None is inherently more important than another, but each requires different skills and gifts. The key is to discern the role God is calling me to fill at any given moment, so I can best choose and use the skills to meet the needs of the people He places before me.

We do not choose our own calling. God chooses it for us. It is God who calls us to a particular situation, family, or profession. Gene Veith writes, "God gives each individual unique talents, skills, and inclinations. He also puts each individual in a unique set of external circumstances, which are understood as having been providentially arranged by God."[1] Daily we seek out the circumstances and opportunities God has "arranged" for us—we listen to our hearts, to family, teachers, pastors, friends, colleagues, and strangers. For me, listening has enormous significance. I have come to believe that it isn't my voice or my parents' or friend's voices that determine what life I live. God speaks His voice into our hearts at Baptism, and it echoes throughout life as we continue to hear Him as He speaks to us in His Word. This continual listening to God's Word in worship and at the Lord's Table enables us to grasp the calling of God that is uniquely ours. To be true to this calling is what it means to live a life of significance.

Often, we mistakenly see our calling only in a future context, as a goal we must achieve ("When I grow up, I want to be a doctor"). Our calling demands a here-and-now focus. It encompasses *today's* tasks: going to class, struggling in a troubled marriage, working a thankless job to pay the bills, caring for a co-worker whose child just died, tending the garden, and paying extra attention to your daughter's friend whose parents are separated. These are all vital callings today. Through the daily routine of our lives, God gives shape to our calling, and thus transforms ordinary life into extraordinary existence.

> Through the daily routine of our lives, God gives shape to our calling, and thus transforms ordinary life into extraordinary existence.

As Christians, we enjoy a distinct advantage as we strive to meet successfully the pressures everyone faces: bills and mortgages to pay, bosses and teachers to satisfy, promotions and acceptance to college to achieve, and parents or grandparents to care for. None of these are easy. By the world's standards, success in any of these areas depends solely on what we do, how much knowledge we attain, and what our neighbors will think. Our measure, however, is taken by *whom* we are: redeemed people of God, called and blessed to live out our calling. In addition to being freed from the weight of societal pressures, as forgiven Christians we are also spared the burden of wondering whether what we do is enough to please God; a consequence of our sinful state is that we will never meet His standards. As Robert Benne reminds us, however, it is God's gift of grace that liberates us from our failed attempts to live up to both worldly and heavenly standards.[2] Through grace the Holy Spirit frees us for a "holy striving" in our life of significance. We continually rediscover who we are as we remember our baptismal call. From this identity flow the works that please God and serve our world. While we want fulfillment in this life, we recognize by faith that our ultimate fulfillment awaits us in the next. For now, we content ourselves with the tasks before us, to humbly don the masks of God in service to others.

It is our duty, then, to relinquish our egos as we focus on serving those God has placed in our path. That means we must possess the humility derived from the profound relationship with our Lord and Savior. For many, this is a difficult step. Fourteenth-century Christian Meister Eckhart laments, "There are plenty to follow the Lord halfway, but not the other half. They will give up possessions, friends, and honors, but it touches them too closely to disown themselves."[3] This is taken from Jesus' own call:

> If anyone would come after Me, let him deny himself and take up his cross and follow Me. For whoever would save his life will lose it, but whoever loses his life for My sake and the gospel's will save it. For what does it profit a man to gain the whole world and forfeit his soul? (Mark 8:34–36)

Discipleship demands that God comes first. As that focus becomes sharper, our own self-importance fades. We decrease so that He may increase.

Self-actualization, and the search for one's self, becomes a moot point for the Christian. As Douglas Schuurman explains, "The point is not to seek one's self—even one's authentic self. The point is to love God and neighbor, and to take up the cross in the self-sacrificial paths defined by one's callings."[4] Or, to paraphrase the great writer Leo Tolstoy, Christian love is merely a preference of others over ones self.[5]

By adhering to the strategies outlined in this book, we are able to move from asking, "How will this benefit me?" to "How will this help those God has placed in my path?" As we are able to diminish and relinquish the needs of our own ego, we naturally discover the life that God created uniquely for us. Terms like "selflessness" and "self-denial" take on new meaning as we discover the paradox that service to Christ and others is what brings fulfillment. By this do we experience daily "the peace of God, which surpasses all understanding" (Philippians 4:7).

Following this path of significance provides us with the freedom to focus our energy on living out the vocational roles that God has planned for each of us. As our relationship with Him deepens, the various roles we fulfill become integrated for service through the open doors God provides. By taking the road less traveled, we, in effect, turn the post-modern world, with its elusive, and ultimately unfulfilling, values, on its head. No longer do we ask, "What's in it for me? How can I get ahead?" Instead, we ask, "How can I be the hands and feet of Christ in this world?" In this way we reflect who we truly are, "a chosen race, a royal priesthood, a holy nation, a people for His own possession" (1 Peter 2:9).[6]

4

THE THREE MISTAKES

A man's steps are from the LORD;
how then can man understand his way?
—**Proverbs 20:24**

Whether we are seventeen or seventy-seven, we human beings fall into ways of thinking and speaking that skew our efforts to live a life of significance. In my experience, there are three mistakes in particular, each of which has to do with our frame of reference in relationship to our calling. The first occurs when we ask, "What do I want to do with my life?" rather than, "What does God want me to do with my life?" When our desires become primary, we inadvertently or maybe even consciously take God out of the equation. At most, He becomes a mere afterthought—window dressing in our conversations. With this in mind, it is worth our while to look closely at how we speak about our goals in life. Statements such as "I want to help people" may indicate a true desire to be of service. But underneath the sentiment may be an attempt to rationalize our ego-driven decisions. It is vital that we not skip the first and most important step in any vocational discernment process—that of strengthening our personal relationship with our Lord and Savior.

The second mistake, which I have already alluded to, occurs when we focus on obtaining some distant future goal: "When I graduate, I want to become a police officer." "When I retire, I want to move to Arizona, play golf, and become involved with charity." Likewise, when our goals remain unfulfilled—seeking a promotion at work, say—we jump to place the blame on someone or something else. "If the 'suits' running this company weren't such idiots, they would listen to my ideas." While responsible planning is one component in our quest to live the life that God intended, our primary focus should always be on the here and now. As will be demonstrated, such a here-and-now focus will, paradoxically, clear the way to discern more clearly how to prepare for the future.

The third misstep happens when our conversations revolve around the *what* in seeking our calling, as opposed to the *how*. When we say, "I want to retire comfortably" or "I want to raise my children so they can be successful in life" or "I want to run for political office," we are making the thing we desire the end goal. This perspective is shortsighted and self-serving. A life of significance is measured by the quality of how we live in the present. "How well have I served my spouse today? How well have I focused on caring for my neighbor? How well have I used my God-given talents at work today?" When we focus on the *what*, we turn inward, making it more difficult to hear God's voice. When we focus on the *how*, we look outward, diminishing our own selves so that the lives of others may be enhanced.

By availing ourselves of the grace God provides around His Word in worship, at the Lord's Table, and in the fellowship of believers, the quality of our living is enriched. By staying connected to Christ, as a branch is to the tree, we can more clearly discern what God has in store for us both today and in the future. We become open to the possibilities and the path He has chosen for us.

5

THE FIRST STEPS
OF OUR JOURNEY

The journey of a thousand miles
begins with one step.
—Chinese Proverb[1]

To grasp our unique calling is one of the most important tasks God gives us. It is a journey that begins at Baptism and continues into eternity. In my experience, two practices have been essential in living a life of significance. These require no special skill—only the discipline to make them a regular part of your daily routine.

First, be intentional about placing your relationship with God at the center of your life—*really*. Take time to pray, study the Word, attend worship, and partake of Jesus' body and blood. From these will flow the second discipline: be aware of ways in which you can attend to others. This requires being present and listening for opportunities of humble service. For example, instead of walking into a colleague's office, craving to share the latest detail of your painful break up, consciously make the effort to inquire about his life. When you're tempted to complain to your adult daughter about your aches and pains, instead tell her about the best thing that happened to you today. Ask yourself, "What is going on in her life? How might I pray for her?" Quietly seek out ways you can be of service to the neighbor who just lost her job. Bring a cup of coffee to your spouse in the morning. Instead of honking at the distracted motorist blocking your lane, say a prayer for God to help her cope with what may be an already overloaded plate. Making a conscience effort to practice these "rituals" leads to a healthier, rejuvenated, contented life. We will discover that doors open, chance meetings occur, and new opportunities arise. We become open to the infinite possibilities of an infinite God. We become less so that we can become more.

We become less so that we can become more.

The journey we have begun is not always smooth or for the faint of heart. We will occasionally relapse, falling into our self-absorbed ways, having to take a step back in order to take two forward. We may, in spirit, say we are ready to make the changes necessary to live a new life, but have yet to discern our true calling. We may make a wrong turn or bump into a closed door. We may allow stress, doubt, and anxiety to block out God's still, small voice. When this happens, and it will, do the following: first, close your eyes and take a deep cleansing breath to clear your mind. Second, say a quick prayer, perhaps something like, "God, please help me discern how, in this moment, to live the life You intend." Third, focus on the here and now. Where are you? What is happening? How will you deal with what is presented to you? *I am in the office. I am in the hospital. I am sitting in class. My spouse and I are having a disagreement. I am at home watching my children.* In your here-and-now circumstance, how might you serve? Let me repeat:

1. Take a deep breath.

2. Say a prayer.

3. Focus on serving someone at this very moment.

By following this or a similar ritual we begin the process of redefining success. We stop being obsessed with all that is wrong, and focus on living the life God created uniquely for us at this particular moment.

There is one caveat before we begin our journey in earnest. Very few, if any, of our callings last a lifetime. We get laid off, we change jobs, we become parents, children grow and leave the house, parents pass away, we get sick. Doors of opportunity open while others close. Our vocations evolve as our life and the world around us changes. While we don't know what the future holds, we know God holds the future in His hands. We know He desires our good, and enables us to discern the life He has created uniquely for us. His Word and Means of Grace stay constant, and He provides forgiveness and strength to meet the needs of others, to be instruments of God's transforming love—movers of mountains. We will, as St. Paul says, *shine as lights in the world.*

Have this mind among yourselves, which is yours in Christ Jesus, who, though He was in the form of God, did not count equality with God a thing to be grasped, but made Himself nothing, taking the form of a servant, being born in the likeness of men. And being found in human form, He humbled Himself by becoming obedient to the point of death, even death on a cross

Therefore, my beloved, as you have always obeyed, so now, not only as in my presence but much more in my absence, work out your own salvation with fear and trembling, for it is God who works in you, both to will and to work for His good pleasure.

Do all things without grumbling or questioning, that you may be blameless and innocent, children of God without blemish in the midst of a crooked and twisted generation, among whom you shine as lights in the world, holding fast to the word of life. (Philippians 2:5–8, 12–16)

Living a life that continually seeks out ways to serve God and to serve someone at this very moment will surprise you, sometimes in unexpected—even unwanted—ways. It will exhaust you physically and emotionally, yet overwhelm you with the peace that transcends understanding. Those who practice worldly values will not always understand or appreciate you, but God will embrace you in the life to come, where He will say, "*Well done, good and faithful servant!*" (Matthew 25:23). It is a journey that as Jesus' disciples we have no choice but to walk, a life that God created uniquely for you and for me.

PART TWO

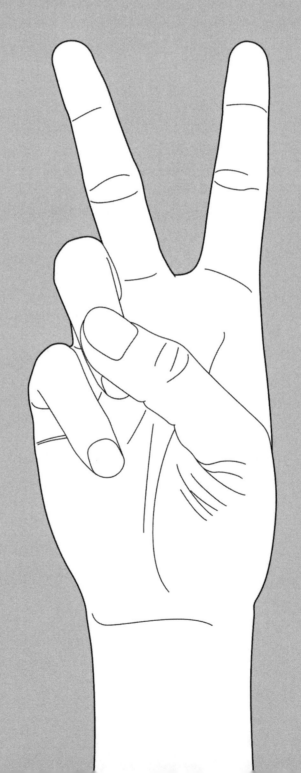

Creating the Road Map: The Strategies

> The meaning of our existence is not invented by ourselves, but is rather detected.
>
> —Victor Frankl[1]

As we continue our quest to discover and live out the life God has called us to, we look intently for helpful strategies, a useful road map, and comprehensive framework to follow. How do we know exactly what God wants us to do today? Whom does He want us to marry? Which career path should we take? For good or bad, most of us won't have the advantage that Noah had when God spoke to him directly. Even if we did, how many of us would react in the same fashion as the classic Bill Cosby routine? The comedian, imitating God, calls out in a deep voice, "Noah! Noah! This is the Lord, Noah!" Noah, nervously responds, "Yeah, right." And, unlike Moses, we probably won't be communicated to by a burning bush. Or like Saul, be struck down on the road to Damascus. This doesn't mean, however, that God does not communicate with us or guide us in the right direction. Recall the prophet Elijah, who hid in a cave while discerning what God wanted him to do next. While in the cave, a great and powerful wind rushed through. After that, he experienced an earthquake and fire. But God's voice was in none of these. Rather, God came to Elijah in *a whisper* (1 Kings 19:11–13).

The Holy Spirit opens our eyes, ears, and hearts to its movement in our lives, as well as enabling us to use secular strategies for faithful purposes. We begin our quest to live out our integrated vocations by exploring and implementing the following eight strategies.

6
THE FIRST STRATEGY

Make God the Center of Your Life

"For I know the plans I have for you,"
declares the Lord, "plans for welfare and not for evil,
to give you a future and a hope. Then you will call upon
Me and come and pray to Me, and I will hear you.
You will seek Me and find Me, when you seek Me with
all your heart." —**Jeremiah 29:11–13**

n my conversations with college students in search of a major, stay-at-home mothers looking for a future calling, professionals unsatisfied in their current job, and retirees wanting new challenges, the question I hear most often is "Where do I start?" My answer is always the same: "Focus first on making God the center of your life." This is the first and most important strategy in our ongoing quest to lead a life of significance. In not making God the center, we run the risk of losing perspective on life in general.

During the Vietnam conflict, Air Force fighter pilot Howard Rutledge was shot down by enemy gunfire and held as a prisoner of war. In his book, *In the Presence of Mine Enemies*, Rutledge tells how he realized belatedly the cost of allowing other priorities to edge God out of the center of his life. He describes that it took prison to show how empty his life was without God, observing, "My hunger for spiritual food outdid my hunger for a steak."[1] Rutledge learned firsthand the wisdom of Jesus' words:

> Therefore I tell you, do not be anxious about your life, what
> you will eat or what you will drink, nor about your body, what
> you will put on. . . . Look at the birds of the air: they neither
> sow nor reap nor gather into barns, and yet your heavenly
> Father feeds them. Are you not of more value than they? . . .
> But seek first the kingdom of God and His righteousness, and
> all these things will be added to you. (Matthew 6:25–27, 33)

Jesus fully comprehends the difference between our cravings and our true needs. The former seeks surface-level, temporary satisfaction; the latter has to do with our soul's needs here and into eternity. To our great detriment we often pay little heed to this spiritual dimension of our lives, which can be satisfied only by a relationship with God. It is in following Him that our lives take on significance. But that is easier said than done.

Our world is full of *noise*, constant distractions that make it difficult for us to hear God's calling. But even hearing does not mean we are *listening*, which results in being obedient and having the courage to accept what God has in store for us. Recall Nicodemus. To the casual observer, it seems he had it all—business success, respect from religious leaders—a real pillar of the community. Deep inside, however, Nicodemus knew something was missing, and he sought out Jesus for help. The answer he got was not what he had expected. "Unless one is born of water and the Spirit, he cannot enter the kingdom of God" (John 3:5). Through our rebirth in Baptism, we become priceless to God; our lives will be restless and empty if we do not, in faith, respond in kind.

> Jesus fully comprehends
> the difference between our
> cravings and our true needs.

This first strategy is simple in theory, yet frustratingly difficult to put into practice. We take our cue from the analogy Jesus uses in the Gospel of John: "I am the vine; you are the branches. Whoever abides in Me and I in him, he it is that bears much fruit, for apart from Me you can do nothing" (John 15:5). John Burke, pastor at Gateway Church in Austin, Texas, reminds us that a branch doesn't have to work all that hard to grow grapes; it merely has to stay connected to the vine.[2]

In our quest to lead lives of significance, we often forget that this first step is not an option. The Bible is replete with commands to keep God at the center of our hearts and lives, the most clear of which is found in the First Commandment, "You shall have no other gods before Me" (Deuteronomy 5:7). Likewise, Jesus says all the commandments are summed up in these words: "You shall love the Lord your God with all your heart and with all your soul and with all your mind" (Matthew 22:37). God will not force Himself on us, but we, as redeemed people, can live God-centered lives in word and deed. In the process, we naturally move from asking, "How do I want to live out my life?" to "How does God want me to live out my life?" There is a shift in perspective here. The self-directed life is a self-centered life focused inward. The life directed by God is other-directed, and focused outward. Put simply, the Christ-filled life is marked by worship of

God and service to the world. In this frame of reference, material possessions, accolades, and fame fade into the background. By staying connected to Christ, as branches to the vine we become more attuned to the "whisper" of God for direction and opportunities to serve.

Our relationship with God is not unlike our relationship with our spouse or best friend. In order for it to grow, we must intentionally and actively communicate with Him. God speaks to us through His Word, through the Sacraments, and through those whom He chooses to use as His instruments. We speak to God through prayer. Initiated by God's gracious act of Jesus' sacrifice on the cross, our relationship with Him is now reciprocal, as we respond to His love and reflect it to the world. In so doing, we fulfill the second part of the Great Commandment—to "love your neighbor as yourself" (Matthew 22:39). The Commandments, then, also become a guide on our journey.

The Letter to the Hebrews instructs, "Let us also lay aside every weight, and sin which clings so closely, and let us run with endurance the race that is set before us, looking to Jesus, the founder and perfecter of our faith" (Hebrews 12:1–2). One way to follow this call is by taking an honest and sometimes painful inventory of our lives to discern the hindrances we must "throw off." I compare this to the monthly cleaning of the refrigerator in the office break room. If we fail to toss out the spoiled food, the stench will only infiltrate the lunch we place in the refrigerator. Likewise, there are parts of our lives that, left alone, have the potential to poison our relationship with God.

Begin by taking an honest inventory of those things, people, and events that are keeping God from being at the center of your life. Your list may be depressingly long. But this is a sign that you are probably being painfully honest! It might include such things as addiction to pornography, prescription drugs, online gaming, or alcohol; a troubled relationship, the need for power, a time-consuming attachment to television, sports, or shopping; an affair, laziness; being impatient, a workaholic, or self-centered, to name just a few. What spoiled garbage is preventing you from deepening your relationship with God? What do you need to humbly ask God to help you with, and what steps can you take to remove these obstacles?

Use the space below to prayerfully and honestly make your personal list:

1. _____

2. _____

3. _____

4. _____

5. _____

6. _____

Now, consider your life in the framework of the following diagram:

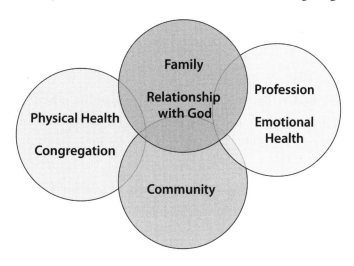

Is this an accurate snapshot of your life? Honestly assess your answer. Notice the integration and balance among the circles. Think about the warning signs that your heart may be off-center: a lukewarm attitude toward worship or hearing God's Word, fear, insecurity, quickness to anger, false idols, or impure thoughts. Begin thinking about what steps you can take so that your life might more accurately be depicted by this idealized diagram.

Why is keeping God at the center so vital to living a life of significance? Thomas Kelly explains:

> We are trying to be several selves at once, without all of our selves being organized by a single mastering life within us. . . . Life is meant to be lived from a Center, a divine Center. Each one of us can live such a life of amazing power and peace and serenity, of integration and confidence and simplified multiplicity, on one condition—that is, *if we really want to.*[3]

Gordon MacDonald adds, God "made us to work most effectively from the inner world to the outer." He concludes by saying that caring for our spiritual life "is a deliberate and disciplined choice a man or woman must make."[4] These observations echo the wisdom of Proverbs, "Keep your heart with all vigilance, for from it flow the springs of life" (4:23).

With God at the center, all else falls into place, and we are truly seeking His kingdom first (Matthew 6:33). In the process, our dutifully scribed laundry list of spoiled garbage miraculously diminishes, and we can see more clearly what God has in store for us. Robert Benne writes, "The Christian life is like breathing in (pulling into our souls the life-sustaining power of the Spirit) and breathing out (expending that life-giving power to others). The Christian life cannot function without both actions."[5]

If, then, we grasp the life-sustaining importance of keeping God at the center of our lives, why is it so difficult to do? Our innate sinful nature, coupled with the pervasive daily bombardment of media-driven messages, seduce us into believing that the path to success is to be prettier, richer, and more powerful. All forms of temptation overwhelm us, and it is not an easy trap to escape. But Jesus puts this challenge and promise to us: "Everyone then who hears these words of Mine and does them will be like a wise man who built his house on the rock" (Matthew 7:24). By returning to our Baptism daily, remaining focused on the Spirit's promise of strength, we become the practitioners Jesus describes, God's "whisper" becomes clearer, and every day becomes an exciting new adventure.

Let me reiterate an important point: God coming into our lives and keeping God at the center of our lives are two different actions. The first action is all God's initiative, completed when He broke down the wall of sin that separated us from Him. The second action doesn't happen automatically; it is something we can only do aided by the power of the Holy Spirit. It is a priority we must strive to make number one, even as we order priorities in life's other activities. We visit the health club to increase our cardiovascular capacity, go to the driving range to improve our golf game, read management books to enhance our leading, or parenting literature to better care for those entrusted to us. So also we "practice" certain strategies—rituals, we might call them—to place and keep God at the center of our lives. We regularly commit a certain time in our day for Bible reading and prayer. We become more active in our church and attend a weekly Bible study. We join a small group at our congregation and/or we attend a local weekly community breakfast Bible study. We hold evening family devotions. We sign up to receive daily devotions by e-mail. We attend an annual spiritual retreat, and maybe listen to biblical/spiritual CDs and tapes while driving.

Rev. John Burke, in his book, *Soul Revolution*,[6] urges us to set our watch, phone, or PDA to beep every 60 minutes for 60 consecutive days. The beep serves as a reminder to snap out of whatever is consuming our time and energy at that moment, and refocus on God. Similarly, my friend Brett Carleton has placed a dot on the face of his watch so that whenever he checks the time he is reminded to keep God front and center. Over time, these rituals become second nature and, in the process, we discover we are experiencing by faith new ways of relating to our Lord and Savior. This grants clarity for our Christian walk. We follow the advice of Paul, who instructs us to "work out your own salvation with fear and trembling, for it is God who works in you, both to will and to work for His good pleasure" (Philippians 2:12–13). We emulate the practice of Jesus, who, "rising very early in the morning, while it was still dark . . . departed and went out to a desolate place, and there He prayed" (Mark 1:35).

Use the following space to list five rituals that you now practice or will implement to deepen your relationship with God.

1. _____

2. _____

3. _____

4. _____

5. _____

The ritual of prayer is vital in our quest to keep God at the center of our life. Paul, in 1 Thessalonians, reminds us to "pray without ceasing" (5:17). What we pray for and how we pray matters. We often pray for worldly things—a new job, good health, better grades, a pay raise. Sometimes we pray for silly stuff, while God would prefer to provide us with things of importance. To paraphrase Martin Luther, we pray for silver, but God would rather give us gold. We may pray for temporary healing, but God wants to provide us with eternal health. The Book of James sternly admonishes, "You do not have, because you do not ask. You ask and you do not receive, because you ask wrongly, to spend it on your passions" (4:2–3).

True prayer is kingdom focused. True prayer asks for forgiveness, humbly focuses on God's Word, asks that God's will be done, and seeks discernment on how to be of service to others. True prayer diminishes our self and focuses on God and others. Using Jesus as our role model, we note that the focus of His High Priestly Prayer prior to His capture by the Roman soldiers was to affirm His oneness with His Father's purpose.[7] And before important decisions during

His public ministry, Jesus retreated to spend time in prayer with His heavenly Father. Gordon MacDonald explains,

> Jesus knew His limits well. Strange as it may seem, He knew what we conveniently forget: *that time must be properly budgeted for the gathering of inner strength and resolve in order to compensate for one's weakness when spiritual warfare begins.*[8]

For us as well, spending time in prayer gives solace and provides us with strength to meet our daily encounters. As our faith grows and matures, as our relationship with God deepens, we will find that we pray more for those around us and less for ourselves. We become intent on praying to live the life that God intended, no matter where the path may lead.

Richard Foster says that when Paul instructs us to *pray without ceasing*, he is reminding us to "seek to discover as many ways as possible to keep God constantly in mind."[9] This means keeping God in mind for others as well as for ourselves. We do this by praying for our spouses and treating him or her the way we would like to be prayed for and treated; praying for and asking our pastor how we can serve him today; and praying and looking for opportunities to serve the co-worker who rubs us the wrong way. Integrating our relationship with God into our daily tasks and relationships is a vital step as we seek to live a life of significance.

By our prayer-filled lives we follow Christ's example, and we are empowered for humble service. When we care for our aging parents, we discover an opportunity both to serve them and enhance our relationship with God. We feel God in our midst when we perform well at work, engage in family game night, tend our garden, unload the dishwasher, or rescue a lost dog. We discover that deepening our relationship with God isn't just another add-on to our overcrowded plate of responsibilities. Instead, it is woven into the very fabric of our daily lives. Brother Lawrence, a seventeenth-century monk, spent most of his daylight hours working in the monastery kitchen in Paris. He cheerfully described his earthly role as the "lord of all pots and pans." He reflects:

The time of work does not differ from the time of prayer. Even in the noise and clutter of my kitchen—when several persons are at the same time calling for different things—I possess God in as great tranquility as if I were on my knees at communion.[10]

Brother Lawrence's devotion, amidst the clanging of his pots and pans, stands as both example and inspiration for us whose lives are filled with so much noise.

God always answers prayer. Jesus Himself gives us His assurance:

And I tell you, ask, and it will be given to you; seek, and you will find; knock, and it will be opened to you. For everyone who asks receives, and the one who seeks finds, and to the one who knocks it will be opened. What father among you, if his son asks for a fish, will instead of a fish give him a serpent; or if he asks for an egg, will give him a scorpion? If you then, who are evil, know how to give good gifts to your children, how much more will the heavenly Father give the Holy Spirit to those who ask Him! (Luke 11:9–13)

Jesus further reminds us, "You did not choose Me, but I chose you and appointed you that you should go and bear fruit and that your fruit should abide, so that whatever you ask the Father in My name, He may give it to you. These things I command you, so that you will love one another" (John 15:16–17).

The love we have for God and the love we have for others is intertwined, leading to humble service to family, friends, colleagues, community, and congregation. We simply cannot find our true calling in life without keeping God at the center.

Connect the Dots

Now there are varieties of gifts, but the same Spirit;
and there are varieties of service, but the same
Lord; and there are varieties of activities, but it is
the same God who empowers them all in everyone.
—1 Corinthians 12:4–6

Our life's calling is providentially arranged. And the Holy Spirit provides us with "signs" to discern what our calling might be. What are our talents, our opportunities, our interests? What messages are family, mentors, and friends giving us? What doors are opening or closing? Are there unexpected tragedies, inexplicable encounters that might give us clues to our calling? Consider the following selection of the Scriptures:

> Having gifts that differ according to the grace given to us, let us use them: if prophecy, in proportion to our faith; if service, in our serving; the one who teaches, in his teaching; the one who exhorts, in his exhortation; the one who contributes, in generosity; the one who leads, with zeal; the one who does acts of mercy, with cheerfulness. (Romans 12:6–8)

> And He gave the apostles, the prophets, the evangelists, the shepherds and teachers, to equip the saints for the work of ministry, for building up the body of Christ. (Ephesians 4:11–12)

It is clear that God knows what gifts He has given us and that He values all gifts equally. Discovering our gifts in order to pursue our calling may be our most important task in this life. Through prayer, listening to others, trying and failing and trying again, we come to identify our gifts. Thus, it is important to be aware of the many factors that influence our calling. When, where, and to whom we are born shapes our calling. The culture in which we live provides us with a certain perspective. What is happening in the economy, even worldwide situations, however remote, have some influence. Daily encounters and experiences profoundly affect what decisions we make and what conclusions we draw. We interview for a job, and it may be offered—or it may not. I ask Laurie to marry me. To my surprise, she accepts. Sydney wins a creative writing competition, and we all celebrate. In our finiteness, we cannot fully comprehend that a divine force helps us unpack the ultimate purpose of our lives. Yet, personal experience convinces us that God, in His infinite wisdom, places others in our paths to help us discover and achieve our goals. With ears, eyes, and hearts open to God's "whisper" we discover the life God has created uniquely for us.

Some people refer to this as *synchronicity*—"a meaningful coincidence that cannot be explained by cause and effect." I prefer my wife's explanation: "It's a God thing." St. Paul puts a finer point on it: "For we are His workmanship, created in Christ Jesus for good works, which God prepared beforehand, that we should walk in them" (Ephesians 2:10). There is a purpose that connects you and me with our fellow sojourners in the Christian life that we don't fully comprehend. On numerous occasions, staff at Lutheran Social Services have excitedly shared, "You aren't going to believe this, but I met this person who . . . " or "It was like God was present, telling me what to say," or "I told a woman where I worked, and she helped me make a connection to a foundation that will support our new project," or "I can't explain it, other than it's just a God thing."

How might we come to appreciate and make the best use of incidences God arranges—the synchronicity—we experience? This is a question of immense significance. We must approach it with prayer and humility so that we don't interpret every minor happening as a "sign from God." At its worst, that is mere superstition. Rather, we are striving to become more attuned to how God works through people, circumstances, and occurrences. The first step is to think about the individuals God has placed in our life from as far back as we can remember—parents, siblings, grandparents, classmates, spouses, mentors, teachers, neighbors, colleagues, strangers, friends, and even those relationships that you would rather forget. It's like connecting links in the chain of our life.

In doing this exercise for myself, I was struck by the array of people—both "saints" and "sinners," from a human point of view—whom God has used to prepare me for a lifetime of service. In making this review, it is difficult to conclude that these relationships were and are merely random. God told the prophet Jeremiah, "For I know the plans I have for you . . . plans for welfare and not for evil, to give you a future and a hope. Then you will call upon Me and come and pray to Me, and I will hear you. You will seek Me and find Me, when you seek Me with all your heart" (Jeremiah 29:11–13). Likewise, God has also set you and me apart, and has a plan for each of us.

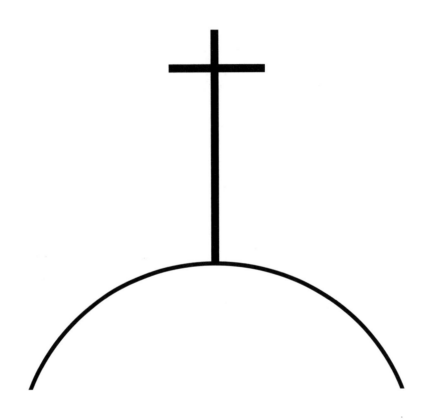

On page 41 is an abbreviated diagram depicting the origins of just a few of the thousands of "dots" that have led me to my current callings.

Now, using the blank diagram on page 42, create your own chart that illustrates who God has placed in your path to bring you to where you are today.

Note the diversity of people, both Christian and non-Christian, God has used in our lives to date. Stepping back, we can see how these dots, which may appear randomly scattered, form a constellation that has given shape to our lives. This gives unique insight not only into how God has acted graciously for us in the past but also into what He might be preparing for the next chapter of our lives.

The next step in coming to recognize God's action through others is to identify those people and organizations who currently inhabit your world. If your chart is like mine, it might include extended family, neighbors, fellow church members, colleagues, clients, stakeholders, friends, people I have met through my volunteer and board activities, neighbors, a waitress at a frequent hangout, members of a health club . . . you get the idea. And this is only the beginning.

Above is a partial depiction of my current world:

On the next page create a diagram that depicts your current world.

When we examine our lives from this perspective, we discover patterns that until now have remained hidden. Within the pattern that emerges, I can see how a neighbor who happens to be a lobbyist may be an important ally toward my goal of passing legislation that will benefit abused children in Texas. It allows me to discover which, if any, of my current personal relationships are obstacles

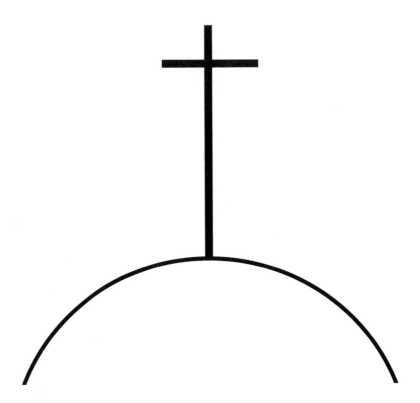

in my effort to keep my life focused on the cross of Christ. It allows me to discern whether a current hobby or volunteer responsibility might be a prelude to assuming a professional role in that arena at a future time. Distinguishing the pattern enhances my service to others as I come to recognize how an acquaintance in one sphere of my life can be of benefit to someone in another sphere, thus enabling both to pursue the life God created uniquely for them.

The connections between the dots in our diagrams are not always easy to see—some are nearly too faint to identify. It may be tempting to force a connection that may not be there, or to manipulate others for selfish interests. The immediate purpose of this exercise is to provide clarity and direction, to give us a birds-eye view of our personal universe; to help us prayerfully pay attention to opportunities to serve those who inhabit the constellation of our life.

The overarching goal is to see the ways in which God has worked through the individuals in our diagram to connect us back to the cross of Christ. This calls for honest reflection: Are the time and energy you expend in your professional role affecting your ability to be a good parent? Are you unconsciously encouraging an unhealthy friendship? What hobbies, addictions, obsessions, or habits are supplanting God from the center of your life?

Take another look at the diagram of your life as you have put on paper. Which dots—relationships—might you want to encourage? Are some blocking your view of the cross? Which could you serve more effectively? Are there any that could benefit from one another by your connecting them? Make your list now. Commit to a date by which you will accomplish this task.

Relationship to be encouraged	Date to be accomplished
1. _____	_____
2. _____	_____
3. _____	_____
4. _____	_____
5. _____	_____

As others contribute to our lives, so we also contribute to the lives of others. Coming to recognize this role is a vital piece of information in our journey; it is part of being a disciple. Jesus poignantly reminds us, "Everyone to whom much was given, of him much will be required, and from him to whom they entrusted much, they will demand the more" (Luke 12:48). In other words, our life of significance is further informed when we appreciate how others might place us as "dots" in their lives. When we act in service to another—being the hands and feet of Christ—we become part of the constellation of the life to which God has called them.

As parents, Laurie and I have the ability to impact Sydney's constellation of dots. This was one of the factors we discussed when choosing to enroll her in a Christian school, for example. We believe God has called us, in our role as parents, to take an active part in helping to shape her life. And we intentionally act and make such decisions that, we pray, God uses for her benefit: worshiping in church and attending youth group; saying no to a party at the home of a friend whose parents we don't know; encouraging and assisting her to get involved in extra-curricular activities like drama and creative writing—those things that help draw out and enhance her God-given gifts. In my role as mentor at work, I am aware of how the relationships of people in my constellation might help a colleague find her professional calling. As a volunteer for Meals on Wheels, Laurie makes a connection between two of the dots she has identified—a client with our pastor. Likewise, God has used one of my friends to connect a neighbor with a church. As an active volunteer and supporter of Lutheran World Relief, I have been privileged to connect a donor with the organization's CEO.

When all is said and done, there may still be doubt—how will I know if I've made the right decision about my calling? I don't subscribe to the view that God has only one professional vocation in mind for each of us, or only one person to become our life's partner, or a particular city where He wants us to end up. That's much too limiting. It could even result in our choices becoming self-fulfilling prophecies. Douglas Schuurman suggests that, in making our decisions, we ask ourselves whether they are part of our desire to serve God and our neighbor, and whether they are made out of gratitude to God and trust in God. If the answer is yes, it matters little whether we choose to become an attorney or a banker, a teacher or a nurse, or marry this individual or that individual.[1]

One benefit of the eight strategies I'm putting forth, including *Connect the Dots*, is that they provide us with tools and constructs that condition us to look inward less and outward more. They provide opportunities to substitute our self-centered ego with selfless empathy for others. They provide openings to detect the "gentle whisper" that tells us which direction our life should take. We become secure in the knowledge that God's hand is evident as we live the life that He created uniquely for you and for me.

Living a life of significance is not an end-game proposition, where starting on the right path guarantees smooth sailing. Neither is it a one-time event, in which our past failures doom us to future disappointment. God's grace and daily forgiveness provide us with a daily do-over, an opportunity to begin the race over and over again. With Christ at the center of our lives, we no longer can be judged by societal standards. You are not a failure if you are passed over for a coveted promotion, or rejected from an Ivy League school. Your success is not determined by whether or not you are in the top ten percent of our nation's income bracket. Overall happiness does not depend on finding the right job or the perfect spouse. What does matter is how well we serve those we encounter. As Christians, we are called to daily *connect the dots* out of gratitude for God's love for us. He calls us not to be successful but to be faithful. That is what it means to lead a life of significance.

God calls us not to be successful but to be faithful.

It is human natures to get frustrated when things do not go our way. Disappointment and doubt settle in when certain dots in our lives do not connect the way we hoped they would. I have seen the look of despair on the face of an interviewee when I have to tell them we do not currently have a need for their skill sets. But, in retrospect, it is often easier to see more clearly why connections in our lives just did not happen. Perhaps a closed professional door may open a door to better serve our family. A family member's serious illness can be devastating, but God can work through it to bring people closer to one another and to Him. We get clearer perspective on how a layoff leads to an opportunity to be of service to others. We come to experience how the death of a child opens us up to be receptive to the love and care of others.

A few years ago, the dots in my life did not connect the way I was sure they would. I was one of the finalists for Chief Executive Officer of Habitat for Humanity International, and thought for sure that this was the calling God had in mind for me. I pursued the position with vigor and excitement. I even convinced my Texas-rooted family that we would enjoy living in Georgia. But God had other plans. He used this experience to help me explore my current calling, to remind me that I wasn't finished fulfilling my role at Lutheran Social Services. God knew better than I how the demands of international travel would have had a detrimental impact on my family life. He knew that Laurie's calling to care for her aging parents was just beginning. He also knew that through this process I would get to know Jonathan Reckford, the person that God had truly called for the Habitat position. Through this connection, Habitat and LSS would develop a close partnership that would effectively serve thousands of Hurricane Katrina survivors along the Gulf Coast. What originally appeared to be a closed door was, in retrospect, another connecting of the dots that served to further God's kingdom.

God is up to something very special for each of us, no matter what our age or stage of life. Before us is a complex galaxy of dots to be connected, and to each of us is given strengths, weaknesses, past baggage, and dreams for the future. The challenge is to humbly inquire and explore how we fit in, to be intentional about using our gifts, doubling the talents God has entrusted to us.

In so doing, we take up the challenge of Professor Keating, in the movie *Dead Poets Society*, to his students; we assume the call to contribute our own unique verse to enhancing God's poetic creation. God is indeed up to something very special, and He will continue to manipulate the events in your life as you live out the life He created uniquely for you. It is our job to be open to the ways God's Spirit works, and to be prepared to take advantage of the opportunities before us.

INCORPORATING RITUALS INTO OUR DAILY LIVES

We are what we repeatedly do.
Excellence, then, is not an act, but a habit.
—Aristotle[1]

n our quest to live a life of significance, we can benefit from research performed with world-class athletes. Jim Loehr and Tony Schwartz started out as consultants to persons such as tennis player Monica Seles, golfer Ernie Els, and basketball great Grant Hill. Over time, Loehr and Schwartz discovered that what works with these athletes also has the potential to impact the lives of more "normal" types, like you and me.

The common theme that emerged from their work is to think of life not as a marathon but as a series of sprints. In their book, *The Power of Full Engagement*, the two researchers describe this process as strengthening our "muscles" in every area of our life. "We must learn to systematically build and strengthen muscles wherever our capacity is insufficient. Any form of stress that prompts discomfort has the potential to expand our capacity—physically, mentally, emotionally, and spiritually—so long as it is followed by adequate recovery."[2] They encourage us to adopt rituals in each life arena, to push ourselves hard for short periods of time, followed by time set aside for rest and rejuvenation, so we can go at it again.

Loehr and Schwartz offer the following questions to determine what rituals we might want to adopt:

1. Define our purpose: "How should I spend my energy in a way that is consistent with my deepest values."

2. Face the truth: "How am I spending my energy now?"

3. Take action: Close the gap between who I am and who I want to be. Create a personal development plan that is grounded in rituals.[3]

In the following pages, I offer suggestions on how to flesh out the authors' questions in ways that will help us in our quest toward leading a life of significance.

Define Your Purpose

How do I want to spend my time and energy in a way that is consistent with my deepest values?

- I want God to be the center of my life.

- I want to live the life that God uniquely created for me.

- I believe that being a mentor to up-and-coming leaders at my workplace is part of my vocational calling.

- I believe God is calling me to actively assist my congregation in fulfilling its mission.

- I want to improve my overall health.

- I want to strengthen my marriage and my relationship with my children.

- I want to get a degree in education so I can serve as a teacher.

- I want to befriend a lonely neighbor in need.

Now, Face the Truth

How am I currently spending my time and energy? Are my daily actions consistent with my purposes as I have defined them? Is there disconnection between who I say I want to be and who I actually am?

Then, Take Action

Take action to close the gap between who I am right now and who I want to be. What rituals can I establish that will help me design a personal development plan?

Example 1

Goal: I want God to be the center of my life.

Truth: My relationship with God is pretty weak. I often skip church. I don't pray regularly. I call on Him only when I'm in trouble.

Action: Rituals I can create:

- ○ Pray daily at prescribed times—when I wake up, before every meal, and when I go to bed.
- ○ Attend church every Sunday and join a weekly Bible study.
- ○ Read Scripture daily.
- ○ Focus on serving those with whom I daily come into contact.
- ○ Avoid acquaintances who are a bad influence.

Example 2

Goal: I want to strengthen my marriage and my relationship with my children.

Truth: I am distracted by work and rarely spend the time I'd like with family.

Actions:

- ○ Set aside one night a week for a date night with my spouse.

- ○ Set aside a block of time every week to do something special with each child.

- ○ Do not check my Blackberry or e-mail the first hour home after work. Instead, focus all my attention on family.

- ○ Become involved in activities that are of interest to other family members.

- ○ Ask them to hold me accountable.

EXAMPLE 3

Goal: I want to improve my overall health.

Truth: I eat too much fast food, don't carve out enough time for exercise, rarely set aside time for prayer and meditation, and occasionally suffer from bouts of depression.

Actions:

- ○ At least two times a day I will eat healthy meals.

- ○ I will schedule four 30-minute segments each week for exercise.

- ○ I will cut my television time by thirty minutes, and devote that time to prayer, devotional reading, and/or meditation.

○ I will engage in at least one act of kindness each day to a stranger, family member, or colleague, and will journal to keep track of each act.

Example 4

Goal: I want to get a degree in education so I can teach children with special needs.

Truth: I have poor study habits. I spend too much time socializing with my friends, hanging out on Facebook, and playing video games.

Actions:

○ I will attend all of my classes.

○ I will block out two hours each day to complete my homework assignments.

○ I will quit my fantasy football league so I have more time to study.

○ I will stop hanging out with those who distract me from my goals.

○ I will focus on making God the center of my life, as I understand the connection between my relationship with God and my desire to live a life of significance.

Loehr and Schwartz's strategy grasps the interwoven nature of life's components. The most effective way to enhance each is to approach life as a series of sprints and to implement rituals that maximize the talents God has given us. As a Christian, what I also find of value in this framework is that it naturally incorporates the need for rest—for Sabbath.

When I work with individuals and groups, I use an exercise designed to have them identify rituals that would work best for them. On a blank piece of paper, I have them draw a number of different-sized circles, and label each with the following: *God, Family, Professional (students might want to substitute Education), Church, Community, Emotional Health, Physical Health, Hobbies, and Time Wasters ("boredom" activities such as watching television, Internet surfing, bar hopping).* Starting with the circles closest to the center of the page, participants identify those that are currently receiving the most focus in their life—using the size of the circle to indicate the amount of time spent on each. Finally, they identify the areas of overlap. If you jog regularly, your *Physical Health* and *Hobby* circles can overlap. Or, if those under your roof hold devotions and attend church together, the *Family* and *God* circles will overlap. For those whose lives are out of balance, their paper might look something like this:

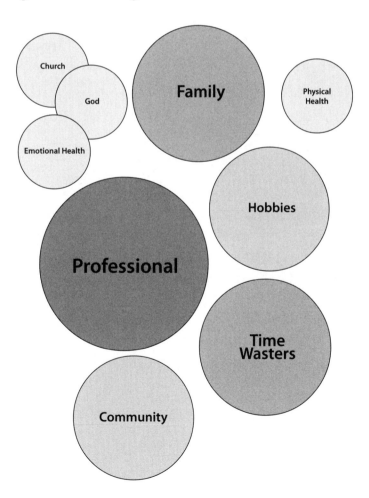

Or, like this:

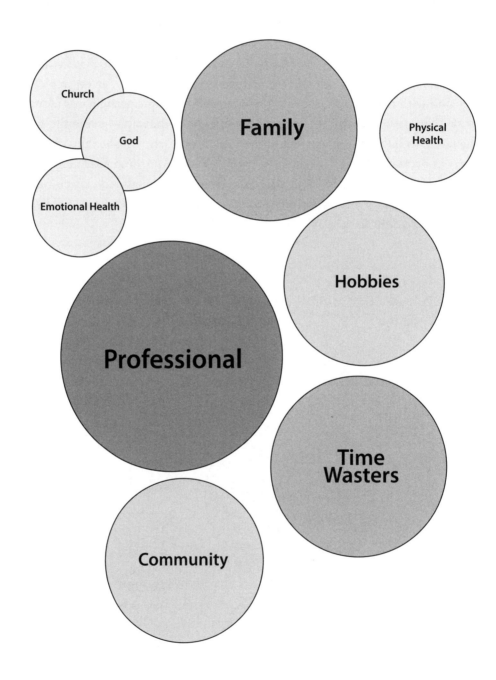

Using the space below, draw your diagram of circles.

There are several aspects of this exercise worth highlighting. First, as you begin "diagnosing" your diagram, ask yourself if the size and location of your *God* circle accurately reflects your current reality. Is your *God* circle at the center of the page? Is it as large as, say, your *Professional* circle, *Hobbies* circle, or even your *Time Wasters* circle? The diagram can be an invaluable, often humbling, tool for identifying how we prioritize our time. In our busy-ness, we may push God out of our daily life, causing the God circle to become smaller and pushed further out toward the page's edge, making it more difficult to discern His will for our life. This is true, even for those of us who spend much of their time in a life of service as relief workers, nurses, pastors, social workers, teachers, and military men and women.

The second observation I make with participants is that their diagram, like life, is not static. The ebb and flow of our circumstances require that we be flexible. My Mondays, for example, tend to have a larger professional circle and a much smaller family circle than, say, my Saturdays or Sundays. Likewise, the nature of my work demands more of my time in October than in December. If that were the case consistently, it would be a clear signal that my life is out of balance, and that I am not living a life of significance.

This exercise is a visual reminder that we may be ignoring or diminishing important roles as children of God. Is our tendency to be self-absorbed pushing to the margins the needs of those around us? Or, do the size and placement of our circles indicate a healthy division of time and energy?

The third aspect of this exercise comes when I ask participants to consider the degree of overlap among circles. More often that not, there is very little. This is a revealing indication of a failure to appreciate the interwoven reality of life. The professional aspect of life is not wholly distinct from the spiritual; engaging in service to community or church benefits us physically, emotionally, and spiritually.[4]

Just as no two people are alike, so no two diagrams will look the same. However, Scripture is instructive in helping us set priorities. The Book of Proverbs describes the characteristics of a certain woman. Thomas Addington and Thomas Graves illuminate:

This woman got high marks from the customers in all the key sectors of her life. In the family area . . . her husband had full confidence in her (Prov. 31:11) and her children called her blessed (v. 28). Her business associates recognized that she was a wise investor (vv. 16 and 18), a conscientious employer (v. 15) and a hard worker (v. 17). In her community, she was known for caring for the poor (v. 20), and she was praised at the city gate for her "works" (v. 31).[5]

It is obvious that this woman lived an integrated life of significance. Below is an example of how our diagrams might look if we were to apply her example to our lives.

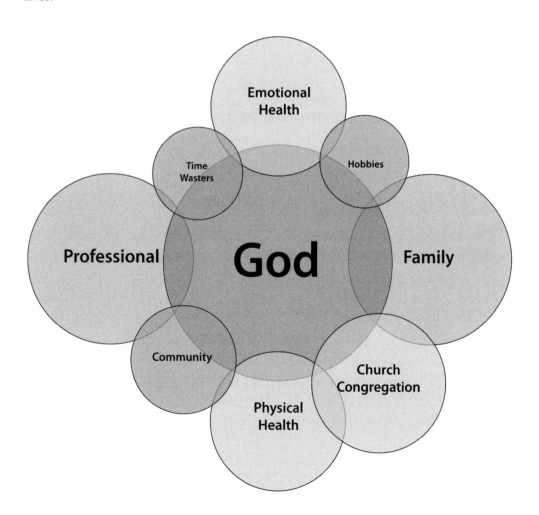

It is one thing to acknowledge that our current lives, as displayed by our circles, may be misaligned. It is a much different task to realign our circles. To do this we need to start by acknowledging our brokenness before God, confessing the sin that keeps ourselves at the center of our lives. It is at the foot of the cross that we find forgiveness for our selfishness, and strength to reorder our life roles. Each one of us (even the one writing a book on this very subject!) daily falls short of living out God's expectations. Recall the wisdom of Thomas Kelly:

> Life is meant to be lived from a Center, a divine Center. Each one of us can live such a life of amazing power and peace and serenity, of integration and confidence and simplified multiplicity, on one condition—that is, *if we really want to*.[6]

It is at the foot of the cross that we find forgiveness for our selfishness, and strength to reorder our life roles.

So, we recognize there is work to do. We must *redraw* our diagram, reprioritize our life with an eye toward accomplishing the following:

- Move our *God* circle to the center of the diagram
- Create overlap among our circles
- Create circles of similar size and importance

Take another look at your diagram. Which circles are smaller or larger than you would like? Which are freestanding? Write down the three goals that you feel will most effectively realign and resize your circles. In other words, what three goals will have the biggest impact in your quest to live a life of significance?

After each goal, write out rituals that will help you achieve your goals. It might look something like this:

Goal 1: Integrate more fully my *God* and *Family* circles.

Rituals to Help Accomplish This Goal:

Pray every night with my spouse.

Ask my children to lead the family prayer at meals.

Attend church as a family every week.

Begin family devotions.

Pray with my child when he or she comes to me with a problem, question, or concern.

Seek to develop friendships with other Christians.

Goal 2: Integrate more fully my *Work* and *God* circles.

Rituals to Help Accomplish This Goal:

Write on a sticky note, "Who can I serve today?" and place it in a visible place.

Be more attentive to a co-worker who is going through a hard time.

Seek out a colleague at work for whom I might be a mentor.

Ask, "How can I add value to the life of a customer or client today?"

Include in my daily prayer those who have specific needs at work.

Set aside a few minutes each day at work for silent prayer.

Join a weekly breakfast prayer group for professionals.

Goal 3: Make my *Community* circle bigger, and make it closer to my *God* circle.

Rituals to Help Accomplish This Goal:

Watch less television and use that time to volunteer at my congregation or a local charity.

Pray daily for a neighbor who is in need.

Tithe to church and/or a worthy charity.

Perform one act of kindness every week for a neighbor or fellow church member.

Determine what I/my family can do to care for the environment— for God's creation.

Next, write out three goals as they relate to the size and/or integration of your circles. List the various rituals you have identified to achieve these goals.

Goal 1:

Rituals: _____

_____

_____

_____

Goal 2:

Rituals: _____

_____

_____

_____

Goal 3:

Rituals: _____

_____

_____

_____

Research confirms the benefits of keeping our various circles balanced and integrated. In a study in which participants were asked to determine those strategies that provide "real, enduring success," for their lives, researchers Laura Nash and Howard Stevenson of the *Harvard Business Review* identified the following necessary components:

Happiness (feelings of pleasure or contentment about your life)

Achievement (accomplishments that compare favorably against similar goals others have strived for)

Significance (the sense that you've made a positive impact on people you care about)

Legacy (a way to establish your values or accomplishments so as to help others find future success)[7]

Nash and Stevenson's research determined that by taking away any one component, we no longer feel we have achieved "real success." For example, if a person devoted all of his time to his career, but did so at the expense of family (Significance) or his ability to enjoy life (Happiness), he would not feel "successful," even if he exceeded expectations at work. Similarly, if one expects to derive happiness by excelling at the office, he or she may feel something is still missing in life.

According to this study, those who enjoyed "real, enduring success" in life had learned how to parcel out time appropriately in each category in order to achieve balance among all four. This task is what Nash and Stevenson labeled "switching and linking"—the ability to "focus intently on one task until it gave them a particular sense of satisfaction, then put it down and jump to the next category with a feeling of accomplishment and renewed energy." These "switchers and linkers" were less likely to attribute their success to a single event, or even a single sphere, of life, and were adept at obtaining a proportionate mix of success in all four areas.[8] Applying this schema to our life as Christians in the areas of family, profession, community, and congregation, we might identify the following: commit to enjoying the moment; seek to solve crucial problems, create real value for others, and do our best to ensure that our actions in each realm will continue to be of value to future generations.

Rituals are important because they help keep us focused. By repetition they become second nature, and can be an effective tool through which the Holy Spirit chooses to move us toward living a life of significance. Being attentive to such regular practices can also help minimize the temptation to indulge in unhealthy habits that harm our relationship with God.

Rituals are vital tool in our effort to enhance, or begin, a behavior we would like to incorporate. It is easier to *act* our way into a new life than it is to *think* our way. As the slogan says, *Just Do It!*, to which I would add, *over and over again!* As the research shows, living out life in periods of intense activity interspersed with periods of rest and solitude proves to be an effective way to use our God-given resources. This ongoing rhythm and flow keeps us rejuvenated, and helps us to appreciate the healing power of our Lord and Savior. Again, Thomas Kelly explains:

> We have hints that there is a way of life vastly richer and deeper than all this hurried existence, a life of unhurried serenity and peace and power. If only we could slip over into that Center! . . . We have seen and known some people who have found this deep Center of living, where the fretful calls of life are integrated.[9]

This is the meaning of living a life of significance.

9
THE FOURTH STRATEGY

Honestly Telling Your Story to Find Your Life

Nobody can go back and start a new beginning,
but anyone can start today and make a new ending.
—**Maria Robinson**[1]

f we are to be truly faithful in living a life of significance, we must assess our
life and tell our "story." Episcopal priest and author Morton Kelsey draws
uncomfortable comparisons between us and some of the characters in the cast
surrounding Jesus' death. Pilate, for instance, says he didn't want to kill Jesus.
Pilate's drive for power, however, was stronger than his drive for justice. He
simply didn't possess the courage to do what was right.

Another actor in the drama is Caiaphas, admired temple leader. Kelsey surmises that the high priest, while sincere, believed he understood the whole truth of the situation, and felt duty-bound to "protect" God from this man, Jesus. Caiaphas proclaimed, "It is good for one man to die instead of a nation being destroyed" (cf. John 11:50). Finally, there was the nameless carpenter who built the cross. He may have known for whom it was intended, but, being a poor man trying to make a living, perhaps justified his labor.[2]

Kelsey, continuing his comparison, talks about that part of ourselves we keep hidden from others—the cellar underneath our public persona where we hide, "the refuse and rubbish which we would rather not see ourselves or let others see."[3] The energy we put into keeping our secrets weakens our resolve to live the life God intended for us. Our tendency is to hold back the full truth of our life story, even when we are whispering it only to ourselves. Each of us must descend the stairs to our personal cellar, open the door, and confront what's inside. Is the timid protection of our status in the face of difficult choices much different from that which Pilate displayed? In justifying behaviors that are less than honorable, do we become "cross makers" of the modern world? Or, in our rigidity and self-righteousness, do we become high priests in the "defense" of our faith? Is our calm exterior hiding a roiling bundle of angst and doubt? More practically, do we proclaim that family is our priority, but spend night after night at the office? Can you look your six-year-old son in the eye and say you will always be there for him, when your high blood pressure, extra weight, and high-stress professional role suggest otherwise?

Jim Loehr, in his book *The Power of Story: Rewrite Your Destiny in Business and in Life* encourages us not only to tell our story honestly, but to rewrite the pages, even chapters, that will transform how we live. Our story encompasses the totality of our life—our physical, emotional, and spiritual health. It encompasses our professional, family, community, and congregational lives; past and present relationships; our faith; material goods; family members; and the lifestyle choices we make in regard to our use of such things as food and alcohol. All these, collectively, make up our story.

Loehr further develops his framework detailing the importance of rituals in a way that adds great value to the quest of living a life of significance. To this end, he urges us to focus on three words: **Purpose—Truth—Action**.

Purpose: What is my ultimate purpose? What am I living for? What principle, what goal, what end? For my whole life and every single day? Why do I do what I do? For what? . . . Have I articulated to myself my deepest values and beliefs, which are the bedrock of who I am and which must be inextricably tied to my purpose (and vice versa). . . . Is my story taking me to where I want to go?

Truth: Is the story I'm telling true? . . . Do I sidestep the parts of my story that are obviously untrue because they're just too painful to confront? [Is] my story honest and authentic or [is] my story made up?

Action: With my purpose firmly in mind, along with a confidence about what is really true, what actions will I now take to make things better, so that my ultimate purpose and my day-to-day life are better aligned? What habits do I need to eliminate? What new ones do I need to breed? . . . Do I believe to my core that, in the end, my willingness to follow through with action will determine the success in my life?[4]

As Christians, we approach these questions from a different point of view. The Purpose, Truth, and Action of our lives flows from our Baptism, and is directed always toward love of God and neighbor. We acknowledge that while we live *in* the world, we are not *of* the world. We are aware that we are sojourners on earth, with heaven our ultimate home. Loehr confirms that when we possess a strong purpose in life, we can do amazing things. "Deep, enduring purpose is virtually always motivated by a desire for the well-being of others."[5] He reminds us that honest storytelling, while difficult, is necessary, lest we suffer the consequences of dishonest storytelling that often surface after the damage is done—when our marriage is beyond repair, we have suffered a stroke or heart attack, or become entombed in our rigidity, cynicism, anger. Tragically, when the story of our lives—and our telling of it—is dishonest and uninspired, it has a deep and painful impact on those closest to us.

Loehr reminds us that the flaws in our stories "simply cannot happen unless we let them happen."[6] We recognize that there are times that negative events will occur in our lives that are beyond our control, for example, our newborn baby succumbs to sudden infant death syndrome, or we are injured in a traffic accident by a wayward driver. However, honesty demands that we recognize the chapters in our personal stories that are capable of and in need of rewriting. We must bear responsibility for our part in how we "let" negative things happen—from being fired to getting caught cheating to suffering a lifestyle-induced heart attack to getting picked up for drunk driving. But we are not as captive to circumstances as we may like to believe; we can change how we live, and thus transform our story.

To that end, Loehr urges us to ask, "In what areas is it clear I can't get to where I want to go with the story I've got?"[7] Honesty demands that we recognize the chapters in our personal stories that need rewriting. This is true of each person, regardless of his or her status, position, or reputation. Dietrich Bonhoeffer, one of my heroes of the faith, acknowledged that he had trouble writing in prison unless he "smokes pretty hard."[8] With what aspects of our story must we struggle? What behaviors and decisions are preventing us from living a life of significance? Only when we answer these questions honestly are we ready to take action to align our behaviors with our purpose.

For this, we call again on the work and wisdom of Loehr, and create rituals to support the story that we want our lives to tell. The most important story is our relationship with God. "Spiritual energy influences the intensity of our stories. It is the energy of purpose, our values and beliefs. It compels us to go beyond ourselves in ways no other energy can, the force behind what we do. This energy defines *why* we are."[9]

Following are examples of how to incorporate rituals to aid us in living a transformed life.

Example 1

I have as my ultimate purpose that of loving God with all my being—to make Him the focus of my days. My current life, however, tells a story of a lukewarm faith that manifests itself in lax worship attendance and half-hearted devotional practices. I can create the following rituals to help align my actions with my ultimate purpose:

Attend church every Sunday, without fail

Read the Bible every morning before going to work

Engage in prayer at specific times and for specific topics. For instance, focus morning prayers for blessing on the day and on those with whom I will interact; noon prayers on thanksgiving and on the needs of others; evening prayers for forgiveness, thanksgiving, and discernment.

Join weekly small-group Bible study

Avoid habits that get in the way of fulfilling my purpose (e.g., use of alcohol, overemphasis on material goods)

Find a person who can mentor me and hold me accountable for choices I make

Pray with my spouse before going to bed every evening

Lead my family in devotion before dinner

Example 2

I have good health as a major purpose, with the goal of playing a significant role in the lives of my grandchildren. My current life, however, tells the story of a two-pack-a-day smoker, who carries around 50 extra pounds and suffers from dangerous cholesterol levels. Rituals for life transformation I might create include:

Exercise from 5:30 to 6:00 a.m. five days a week

Make each weekday alcohol-free, and limit myself to two glasses of wine on weekends

Be in bed by 10 p.m. on weekdays

Cut out all fast food; take lunch to work

Use the stairs at work rather than taking the elevator

Turn off Blackberry and computer by 8 p.m.

Eat a combination of five vegetables and fruits daily

Start each day with a healthy breakfast

Schedule a physical exam and commit to telling my physician everything

Example 3

I have as my purpose to be an active participant in co-creating a healthy, God-pleasing marriage and Christian home for our children. My current story, however, is characterized by a too-busy life at work that leaves little energy or time for spouse and family. Rituals I can create that will help me reach my purpose, and thus rewrite my story to have a happier ending, include the following:

A weekly date night with my spouse

When possible, limit travel to no more than two overnight trips a week

Spend time in an uninterrupted activity with each child or
grandchild at least once a week

Call each family member who lives out of town once a week

Attend church with family every week

Eat together as a family at least four evenings a week

Take a family vacation at least once every two years

Attend a marriage retreat

Seek counseling for depression

Example 4

I have as a life purpose to be an effective leader and mentor for those
who report to me at work. The current reality is that much of my time is
consumed reacting to "emergencies," which results in little face-to-face time
with employees. Rituals I can adopt to help meet my stated purpose include the
following:

Engage in in-depth conversations with each direct report to review
their one-, five-, and ten-year goals

Create and implement a leadership development program for
each direct report

Praise staff for a job well done

Model a balanced life

Follow the golden rule in shaping organizational culture

Hold difficult conversations with employees in person only

Make daily rounds to check in with staff

Don't ask an employee to do something you are not willing to do
yourself

Through conscious repetition and by intention, our rituals become healthy habits and, thereby, help shape a new life story. We are then free to work on enhancing our story in other important ways.[10]

None of our stories are perfect. Some of the flaws in the world and in our lives are the result of sin, though not necessarily our own actual sin: the veteran, for example, who returns from war without a limb, the child with Tourette's syndrome, or the young adult battling with the challenges of being bi-polar. Yet each of us also possess flaws because of our personal sins. There are misplaced chapters, unhappy endings, broken sentences, and a deeply flawed main character. Self-centeredness, a failing marriage, and a host of unnamed—perhaps unrealized—preoccupations and addictions contribute to a story line that is often less than wholesome, and, at times, twisted. Fortunately for us, God's story is wrapped around our own. Jesus has fulfilled God's requirement of perfection. Because of His sinless and sacrificial life story, we become a new creation. Each day brings the opportunity to begin a new story, one of service to God and neighbor, one marked by honesty, health, and integrity—all made possible through the grace of a forgiving and empowering God.

> Each day brings the opportunity to begin a new story, one of service to God and neighbor, one marked by honesty, health, and integrity.

Drawing from the wealth of research referenced above, and by sharing personal experiences, I have tried to show that the rituals we incorporate are an effective means for re-creating our life story. But rituals are good only if we actually carry them out. This requires a system of accountability. One way that has proven to be successful in this is to invite another person to be your accountability partner. He or she agrees to connect with you regularly (once or twice a week) to discuss whether you are keeping your rituals. You can also hold yourself accountable through a daily log by which you track your progress.

Use the space below to write out two aspects of your personal story that you would like to transform. Then list the rituals that will help achieve that transformation, as well as the habits you need to eliminate in order to bring your purposes and *how you are currently living* into alignment. Finally, write down how you will hold yourself accountable.

Story Line 1 That Needs Revising:

_____

_____

_____

Rituals That Will Help Rewrite This Story Line:

_____

_____

_____

Accountability Mechanism:

_____

_____

_____

_____

Story Line 2 That Needs Revising:

_____

_____

_____

_____

Rituals That Will Help Rewrite This Story Line:

_____

_____

_____

_____

Accountability Mechanism:

_____

_____

_____

_____

THE TWO CURVES

Commit your work to the LORD,
and your plans will be established.
—Proverbs 16:3

A couple of years ago, Laurie and I were invited to join a group that was spending part of an afternoon with Jimmy and Rosalyn Carter in their Plains, Georgia, home. We were struck by the commitment and vibrancy of this couple who, even in their eighties, continue to focus on living a life of significance. They remain active in their local Baptist church; active with *The Carter Center*, where research has helped eradicate guinea worm disease, find a cure for river blindness and malaria, and ongoing advocacy on behalf of human rights and fair elections around the world; active with the work of Habitat for Humanity in making affordable housing available for low-income individuals; as well as a host of volunteer activities. No matter what your political leanings, the Carters serve as role models for us all.

President Carter shared a story with us, drawn from the prelude to his book, *Why Not the Best?* Carter recalls:

> I had applied for the nuclear submarine program, and Admiral Rickover was interviewing me for the job. It was the first time I met Admiral Rickover, and we sat in a large room by ourselves for more than two hours, and he let me choose any subjects I wished to discuss. Very carefully, I chose those about which I knew the most at the time—current events, seamanship, music, literature, naval tactics, electronics, gunnery—and he began to ask me a series of questions of increasing difficulty. In each instance, he soon proved that I knew relatively little about the subject I had chosen.
>
> He always looked right into my eyes, and he never smiled. I was saturated with cold sweat.
>
> Finally, he asked me a question and I thought I could redeem myself. He said, "How did you stand in your class at the Naval Academy?" Since I had completed my sophomore year at Georgia Tech before entering Annapolis as a plebe, I had done very well, and I swelled my chest with pride and answered, "Sir, I stood fifty-ninth in a class of 820!" I sat back to wait for the congratulations—which never came. Instead, the question: "Did you do your best?" I started to say, "Yes sir," but I remembered who this was, and recalled several of the many times at the Academy when I could have learned more about our allies, our enemies, weapons, strategy, and so

forth. I was just human. I finally gulped and said, "No sir, I didn't always do my best."

He looked at me for a long time, and then turned his chair around to end the interview. He asked one final question, which I have never been able to forget, or to answer. He said, "Why not?" I sat there for a while, shaken, and then slowly left the room.[1]

No matter what our age or station in life, God calls us to use our talents and abilities on behalf of others. To paraphrase President Carter, why not give God the best of what we have to offer?

No matter what our age or station in life, God calls us to use our talents and abilities on behalf of others.

Carol Dweck, in *Mindset: The New Psychology of Success*,[2] demonstrates that individuals succeed or fail based on their estimation of their own intelligence. She proposes that people approach life from one of two mindsets. First, there are those who have a "fixed" mindset. These people will avoid challenges, are threatened by the potential of negative feedback, are afraid to learn or teach from a new paradigm, and will generally exert less effort in life. Ironically, one can be very talented and yet operate with a fixed mindset.

Then there are those who possess what Dweck calls a "growth mindset." People who fall into this category believe that intelligence, like a muscle, can be developed. Research indicates these people are more likely to push themselves more, despite the risk, and that they embrace criticism because they believe it will ultimately make themselves better people. Individuals with such a mindset perceive hard work as a path to mastery, and look forward to being evaluated by their peers.

The Two Curves

We human beings go through our days in what I call a *natural life cycle*. Like a roller coaster car, we grow and mature as we enjoy the ride to the top. As we age, however, and perhaps endure the painful consequences of our inaccurate storytelling, the ride down becomes dramatic and steep. We can prevent an out-of-control plummet, however, by continually reinventing ourselves—by having a growth mindset. This keeps us fresh so that, as our car teeters at life's pinnacle, we can switch tracks, avoid the downward plunge, and continue to enjoy the ascending ride. From this vantage point, we can live fully in the present and simultaneously create a future life marked by faithful service to God and others.

Our life cycle can by symbolized by the S-shaped Sigmoid Curve depicted below.

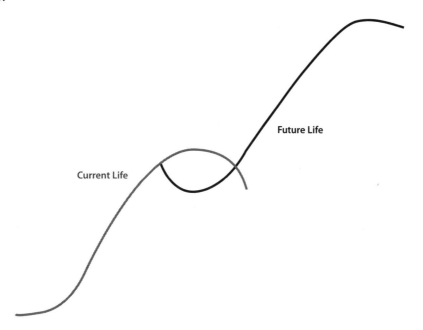

The corporate world has used this concept as a way to adapt to changes within and beyond the organizational environment. Organizations that plan from this perspective pay attention to where they are located on the *present* curve, and at the same time, plot the shape and details of their *future* curve.[3]

Consider for a moment the nature of your roller-coaster ride. A typical ascent might include a series of accomplishments—expanding your social circle, gaining education through high school and college, growing in your Christian faith, enhancing your skill set for your career, and feeling the excitement of first-time parenthood. But, at some point, complacency sets in. Your drive to learn plateaus and your spiritual walk feels more like running in place. You lose interest in keeping up with developing technology, perhaps relying instead on your children to do the troubleshooting. You find yourself reminiscing for the good old days, rather than embracing the power of the new. But all this need not be so.

A life viewed from a present-and-future vantage point means we can adapt and adjust. Children leaving home, a sudden job ending, the onset of serious disease—these need not lock us into a predetermined future. Instead, we can live fully in the moment *and* create our future. This is possible as we draw from the past, when God created us anew in Baptism and set us on a curve of hope.

As I consider my own *natural life cycle*, I see that, at present, the curve of my professional life includes leading a $90 million multi-state nonprofit organization and serving as Chairman of the Board of a *Fortune 500* enterprise. While fulfilling these roles to the best of my ability, I am also focused on keeping my skill sets sharp so that, as changes come (and they will!), I can adapt. At the same time, I am praying for discernment about what God has in store for me five or ten years from now. Not knowing what that will be, or what will be required, I continue to hone my skills in writing, teaching, public speaking, technology, and consulting. I am intentional about reviewing the rituals that will help me both maintain my current goals, as well as create new ones that will be required.

In terms of my personal and family path, Laurie and I are focused on our *present* and *future* curves as they relate to our shared vocation as a family. What decisions are necessary today that will prepare us to be effective and compassionate caregivers for our aging parents? What additional volunteer and/ or professional roles does God have in store for Laurie when Sydney no longer needs as much of her time and energy, and how then should she continue to enhance her skill sets today to meet those needs? How can she and I be better stewards of our resources today to ensure that Sydney, our grandchildren, our congregation, and other important ministries continue to be cared for in the future?

In the same vein, Sydney, and our nieces and nephews, are focused on their high school, college, and graduate studies today in order to create a vibrant future curve of service to others in their future professional callings. At the same time, they also remain "in the moment," as they care for their grandparents, help friends in need, participate in church and youth groups, go on mission trips, serve customers in their part-time work, and listen to and respect their parents.

There is good scriptural support for a present-and-future oriented life perspective. Paul puts it succinctly: "Do not be conformed to this world, but be transformed by the renewal of your mind, that by testing you may discern what is the will of God, what is good and acceptable and perfect" (Romans 12:2).

Following are rituals I have recently implemented as I live out my present curve *and* prepare for my future curve:

1. Commit to understand and utilize today's technology, both at home and at work.

2. Seek and accept offers to write and speak.

3. Devote time to learning more about Sydney's interests.

4. Commit time to volunteer and support the ministries of Lutheran World Relief in my growing desire to broaden my interest and service to those outside the United States.

5. Devote time to reading anything and everything that pertains to leadership, vocation, third-world policies, scientific research, finance, history, sociology, technology, future trends, and, of course, my Christian walk.

Below, list those rituals that are currently a part of your life, or that you will implement to prepare you for tomorrow:

1. _____

2. _____

3. _____

4. _____

5. _____

What we do today impacts how we live out the life God has created uniquely for us. If, during college, we lean more toward the social scene and less toward academics, chances are we will be ill-prepared to meet opportunities for service when we encounter them. If we ignore our health today, we may not have the physical or emotional resources to be of service to others tomorrow. If, today, we pay little attention to the state of our spiritual health, we may find we lack a sense of meaning and purpose necessary to meet the crises of tomorrow—the loss of a loved one, a troubled marriage, or a natural disaster.

A present *and* future life perspective helps us avoid the pitfall of seeing God's full plan for us as something yet to be realized or as a hazy distant goal we are driven to attain. As God's baptized, we live beneath the umbrella of grace: renewed for service today, curious about and empowered for service tomorrow.

As God's baptized, we live beneath the umbrella of grace: renewed for service today, curious about and empowered for service tomorrow.

We sometimes excuse ourselves from personal responsibility and growth by believing our lives are determined by our biology. Geoff Colvin, in *Talent Is Overrated*,[4] would remind us differently. He proposes that genetics play a small role in determining whether we achieve our goals in life. He argues that one of the greatest predictors of success is a disciplined focus—a willingness to create a deliberate practice in our relentless effort to improve ourselves. Colvin cites Jerry Rice as an example of such relentless pursuit of excellence. The Hall of Fame pro-football receiver overcame average size and speed by focusing on increasing his endurance. This reserve of energy gave him the winning advantage when, late in the game, his defenders tired.

Do we have rituals that are effective in meeting our goal to double the talents God has entrusted to us? Are we focusing on our present curve for us to effectively employ our gifts in the future? Malcolm Gladwell, author of *Outliers: The Story of Success*, relates findings by researchers who studied violinists at Berlin's elite Academy of Music. Students were separated into three groups: the "stars," who had the potential to become world-class soloists; those determined to be merely "good"; and a third group, composed of those who were unlikely ever to play professionally but were destined to teach music in the public school system. Researchers found a direct correlation between which group violinists were assigned to and the accumulated hours each had spent practicing over time. The "stars" had practiced, on average, a total of ten thousand hours, the "good" students, by contrast, totaled eight thousand, and the future music teachers had practiced for a total of only four thousand hours.[5]

This study yielded the surprising conclusion (one supported by other research) that there were very few "natural" musicians, that is, those who came by their stardom without investing heavily in practice. Instead, their study revealed that a distinguishing factor that determined a person's level of expertise is the degree to which he or she was willing to work for it.

Similar observations have been made by others. Neurologist Daniel Levitin writes:

> The emerging picture from such studies is that ten thousand hours of practice is required to achieve the level of mastery associated with being a world-class expert—in anything. In study after study, of composers, basketball players, fiction writers, ice skaters, concert pianists, chess players, master criminals, and what have you, this number comes up again

and again. Of course, this doesn't address why some people get more out of their practice sessions than others do. But no one has yet found a case in which true world-class expertise was accomplished in less time. It seems that it takes the brain this long to assimilate all that it needs to know to achieve true mastery.[6]

Is your calling to be a public speaker? Follow the path of self-help guru Tony Robbins, who talks about how early in his career he would set up two to three speaking engagements *each day*. He realized that to be successful in the future required constant practice today.[7] Want to be an effective writer? Heed the advice of one of my law professors who urged me to write as often as possible—in class, for the school newspaper, journals, and magazines (all for free!)—so that someday I could write professionally. The same principle applies in every area of life. Want to have a healthy, loving family? Make the commitment today to set aside time for your spouse and children. Want to live a life in which you feel satisfied and fulfilled? Make the commitment today to create and integrate rituals to aid you in your spiritual journey.

Thrivent Financial investment advisor Darrell Shideler consistently makes the bold claim that we can never realize the full potential of the talent God gives us. If we accept that claim, it follows that every day is an opportunity to improve. My friend John Nunes urges me to focus on meeting at least one new person every day. In so doing, I enlarge my constellation of dots, so that my life of service can have a greater impact. I have found that the advice of these two friends has been invaluable in my personal goal to "double the talents" God has given me.

Before getting into the next chapter, I want to put into proper perspective once again the nature of the principles I am setting forth in this book. My references to the need for self-improvement by practice, the goal of realizing our potential, of creating our future, and other related emphases, should not be understood as activities to be undertaken as exercises we can accomplish solely by or for ourselves: I stated in the introduction that this is not just another self-help publication.

Every principle I propose within these pages is offered in the full realization that none of our efforts can improve our standing before God. Rather, I suggest them as methods through which the Holy Spirit can work to help us in our sanctified walk with God. It is in that spirit that we begin the next chapter, wherein I address the pursuit of happiness and success.

II
THE SIXTH STRATEGY

The Power of Flow

Don't aim at success—the more you aim at it
and make it a target, the more you are going to miss it.
For success, like happiness, cannot be pursued; it must
ensure . . . the unintended side-effect of one's personal
dedication to a course greater than oneself.
—**Victor Frankl**[1]

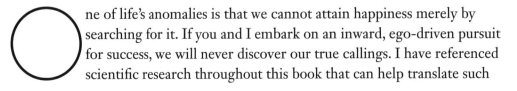

One of life's anomalies is that we cannot attain happiness merely by searching for it. If you and I embark on an inward, ego-driven pursuit for success, we will never discover our true callings. I have referenced scientific research throughout this book that can help translate such scriptural insights into twenty-first-century terms. We turn to University of Chicago psychology professor Mihaly Csikszentmihalyi's exhaustive study that serves as the basis of his book *Flow: The Psychology of Optimal Experience*. This seminal work shows that the path to a sense of personal fulfillment is through purposeful challenge. This is in contrast to the worldly emphasis on mindless hedonism. Drawing from his study, which spans two decades, the author demonstrates that the meaningful activities in which we engage have a direct impact on the degree to which we feel our lives have purpose. Through such engagement, participants in the study lived life with a mindset he calls *flow*.

Flow is defined as "the state in which people are so involved in an activity that nothing else seems to matter; the experience itself is so enjoyable that people will do it even at great cost, for the sheer sake of doing it."[2] Csikszentmihalyi demonstrates that achieving *flow* does not depend on health, wealth, or position in life. Rather, a more accurate predictor is whether an individual perceives external challenges as opportunities for action or as debilitating threats. It is by seeing challenge as opportunity whereby any activity becomes intrinsically rewarding to an individual. You and I hear about this *flow* mindset daily—and, I hope, share the same. A surgeon says she finds her work so rewarding, she would do it even if she weren't paid. Athletes talk about being "in the zone" while competing. The owner of a vineyard finds the enjoyment of being in God's creation doing her work is rewarding in its own right, whether or not her wine sells. And, for many social workers, pastors, teachers, and other caregivers, *flow* is an important factor that keeps them committed, despite the low pay.

The importance of focusing on meaningful tasks also brings order to the chaos that otherwise characterizes our mind, according to Csikszentmihalyi. Without attention to task or goal, we are unable to focus on the present for more than a few minutes at a time:

> But when we are left alone, with no demands on attention, the basic disorder of the mind reveals itself. With nothing to do, it begins to follow random patterns, usually stopping to consider something painful or disturbing. Unless a person knows how to give order to his or her thoughts, attention will

be attracted to whatever is most problematic at the moment: it will focus on some real or imaginary pain, or recent grudges or long-term frustrations. Entropy is the normal state of consciousness—a condition that is neither useful nor enjoyable.[3]

This, in part, explains why some aging adults talk—sometimes randomly, it seems—about their aches and pains. The same principle applies to how we spend our time. Watching television, unlike reading or engaging in a hobby, takes a very little investment of psychic energy. Most people, according to Csikszentmihalyi, say that not only do they have nothing to "show" for the time they spend in front of the television screen but also report "feeling passive, weak, rather irritable, and sad."[4] He argues that the path to fulfillment is to embrace activities that are enjoyable and make the self grow.[5] The author admonishes, "Unless a person learns to enjoy (solitude), much of life will be spent desperately trying to avoid its ill effects."[6]

Csikszentmihalyi's writing suggests that, while he may be agnostic in terms of his worldview, he readily acknowledges that having a traditional faith that informs our life provides a connecting order between flow activities and an overall context that provide meaning to the myriad of events that make up our everyday life.[7]

Our relationship with God through faith in Jesus Christ provides the "connecting order" that transforms our life into a single *flow* activity. The cross of Christ provides the framework for a life flow, a life of forgiveness and wholeness, of flow connecting the "tasks" and blessings of work, worship, and service to others.

....

The cross of Christ provides the framework for a life flow, a life of forgiveness and wholeness, of flow connecting the 'tasks' and blessings of work, worship, and service to others.

Keeping that vital reminder in mind, we turn now to the steps Csikszentmihalyi proposes by which our daily activities become part of our life's flow:

- **One must establish clear goals.** Once a goal is defined, challenges and a series of actions are defined to accomplish the goal. "The pursuit of a goal brings order in awareness because a person must concentrate attention on the task at hand and momentarily forget everything else."[8]

- **Become immersed in the activity.** Whether it is washing dishes or writing a novel, a person into the flow of life is deeply immersed into what he is doing.

- **Pay attention to what is happening.** Become wholeheartedly committed to achieving your goals. For example, a parent who does not focus all of her attention on her child will undermine that particular interaction. A basketball player who gets distracted by the crowd will miss the free throw.

- **Learn to enjoy immediate experience.** The outcome "of learning to set goals, to develop skills, to be sensitive to feedback, to know how to concentrate and get involved—is that one can enjoy life even when objective circumstances are brutish and nasty. Being in control of the mind means that literally anything that happens can be a source of joy."[9]

From Csikszentmihalyi's perspective, "it does not matter whether one volunteers with the Cub Scouts, participates in a group exploring the Great Books, works toward preserving the environment, or supports the local union. What counts is to set a goal, concentrate one's psychic energy, pay attention to the feedback, and make certain that the challenge is appropriate to one's skill. Sooner or later the interaction will begin to hum and the flow experience follows."[10]

To help place these insightful recommendations into the context of living a life of significance as God's people, I suggest the following:

- Implement rituals that will keep God in the center of your life. Focus on discerning on how He wants you to serve today and in the future.

- Establish clear and specific tasks for how you will serve in your family, professional, community, and congregational roles.

- Become totally immersed in those tasks, mindful that they flow from God's grace, through you, to reach others by your unique talents.

- Be completely focused on the present moment, knowing that that the specific opportunity will present itself only now, and only in this way.

- Learn to enjoy the immediate experience, knowing that we are indeed sinners and saints, broken and forgiven.

Experiment with these suggestions over the next few days. See if, by bringing your best to the present moment, fully appreciating the uniqueness of the task, you are able to better enjoy your work, be it washing the dishes, playing board games with your children, tending your garden, shoveling snow, studying for tomorrow's algebra exam, or going to the grocery store. See if the same mindset also transforms your attitude toward less enjoyable situations like a difficult employee evaluation, or the repetitious, but necessary, tasks at work. Even these can become purposeful and meaningful.

As an example, in the week following the time I was writing these words, I was faced with the tasks listed below, and committed to approaching each as an opportunity for service to God as they presented themselves:

1. Clean up the "presents" left in our backyard by our border collie.

2. Pick up our daughter and her friends from the high school football game.

3. Think how I can help make a less-than-satisfactory employee review a means of growth for that person.

4. Give laser-like attention to our daughter when she wants to talk.

5. In preparation for the upcoming board meeting, identify one member who can use additional acknowledgment, a listening ear, or a prayer.

Take time now to list five activities on your "to do" list this week that you can commit to approaching with full attention, and which you can appreciate as opportunities to serve:

1. _____

2. _____

3. _____

4. _____

5. _____

This approach also helps moderate our ego—that part of us that, left unchecked, strives for personal attention, for the desire to lift ourselves up, often at the expense of others. Our egos are behind the need to stand out, to be in control, and to accumulate power. Eckhart Tolle, like Csikszentmihalyi, is straightforward in his estimation of the human brain: "Recognize the ego for what it is: a collective dysfunction, the insanity of the human mind."[11]

When we are unmindful of our special status as God's baptized, it is easy to live in the "insanity" of our sin. Our days become a meaningless bunch of hours, we lose sight of the importance of our relationship with God, and we begin justifying lax behavior and attitudes toward work and those we love; God decreases, in our estimation, and ego increases. Rather than denying ourselves and taking up our cross, as Jesus demands, we live with what Tolle calls an "illusion of self."[12]

By contrast, the life of discipleship is a life in proper alignment, of the transformed and renewed mind of Christ, of the order that true peace brings—not the chaos of the world that results in selfishness.

God works through the Holy Spirit to keep our ego in its proper place. From the vantage point of our faith we are able to grasp the ethical demands of Jesus: "And if anyone would sue you and take your tunic, let him have your cloak as well. And if anyone forces you to go one mile, go with him two miles" (Matthew 5:40–41). Or, "When you are invited, go and sit at the lowest place, so that when your host comes he may say to you, 'Friend, move up higher.' . . . For everyone who exalts himself will be humbled, and he who humbles himself will be exalted" (Luke 14:10–11). And, "Blessed are the poor in spirit, for theirs is the kingdom of heaven" (Matthew 5:3).

True *flow* flows from the waters of our Baptism, in which we were created for lives of service. We cooperate with the Holy Spirit to set goals and establish rituals to reach them. We step each day into the life of significance God created uniquely for us.

12
THE SEVENTH STRATEGY

LEADING A LIFE OF SIMPLICITY

The lack of wealth is easily repaired,
but the poverty of the soul is irreparable.
—Montaigne[1]

The world would have us believe power, wealth, beauty, and sexual pleasure are the keys to finding happiness. William Placher places such worldly values in stark contrast to those Jesus places before us, and which call us to ask, "What is God calling me to do?" "How can I pick up my cross and follow Jesus?" We dare not minimize these questions, for they place before us our reason to struggle against the seemingly overwhelming societal forces.[2]

It is easy to get caught up in striving for what the world considers valuable—those *things* that bring happiness. I referred in the sixth strategy to Eckhart Tolle's call to be wary of the selfish nature of the human ego, particularly in relation to *things*. He says we possess an "unconscious compulsion to enhance one's identity through association with an object."[3] The advertising industry, through persuasive marketing, tells us how we can enhance our sense of self: we will stand out from the crowd in the latest fashions; be successful behind the wheel of a luxury car; turn back the clock of time with expensive skin creams; and enhance our athletic abilities by using celebrity-endorsed products. Tolle refers to designer labels as "identity enhancers," and observes:

> Paradoxically, what keeps the so-called consumer society going is the fact that trying to find yourself through things doesn't work: The ego satisfaction is short-lived and so you keep looking for more, keep buying, keep consuming. . . . Ego-identification with things creates attachment to things, obsession with things, which in turn creates our consumer society and economic structures where the only measure of progress is always more. The unchecked striving for more, for endless growth, is a dysfunction and a disease.[4]

Deion Sanders, former professional football and baseball standout, gives astute advice to those he mentors: "Never love something that doesn't have the capacity to love you back—whether it's a mansion, a Ferrari, or a diamond watch. It (sports) can pay your bills and give you stardom and fame, but it can never love you back. It doesn't have a heart."[5] Tolle elaborates on this theme when he says, "You can value and care for things, but whenever you get attached to them, you will know it's the ego."[6] An ego-driven attachment to material goods is directly opposed to Jesus' call to discipleship—to a life of significance. The evangelist Luke relates a parable in which a man approaches Jesus with a very human demand:

> "Teacher, tell my brother to divide the inheritance with me."

In His concluding observation, Jesus warns:

"Take care, and be on your guard against all covetousness, for
one's life does not consist in the abundance of his possessions.
. . . Therefore I tell you, do not be anxious about your life,
what you will eat, nor about your body, what you will put on."
(Luke 12:13, 15, 22)

In the parable of the rich fool, Jesus sets forth even more clearly how placing
our security in the gathering of human things puts our soul in danger:

The land of a rich man produced plentifully, and he thought
to himself, "What shall I do, for I have nowhere to store my
crops?"

And he said, "I will do this: I will tear down my barns and
build larger ones, and there I will store all my grain and my
goods. And I will say to my soul, Soul, you have ample goods
laid up for many years; relax, eat, drink, be merry."

But God said to him, "Fool! This night your soul is required
of you, and the things you have prepared, whose will they
be?"

So is the one who lays up treasure for himself and is not rich
toward God. (Luke 12:16–21)

It is beyond question, from a scriptural perspective, that consumerism is an
impediment in our quest to "leave everything behind" in order to follow Jesus. A
Christ-centered life is not necessarily one of material poverty. Rather, it is a life
in which all possessions and relationships have value only when we understand
them as gifts from God, and by which we serve God. The sacrifice of Jesus as the
most precious gift enables us to live a life of simplicity, and helps us understand

that we are truly *in* the world but not *of* the world. We are freed from having to follow the path of accumulation—a life of loneliness and spiritual poverty—and instead gifted with a spirit of radical generosity and service.

The difficult truth, however, is that the wealthier we are, the harder this can become. *Wall Street Journal* writer Robert Frank, observes, "The wealthy seem to be as besieged as ever . . . an elite of BlackBerry-crazed, network-obsessed, peripatetic travelers who have to keep scrambling to keep their place in life."[7] Nobel Prize-winning behavioral economist, Daniel Kahneman, adds, "Being wealthy is often a powerful predictor that people spend less time doing pleasurable things and more time doing compulsory things and feeling stressed."[8]

We become so focused on making "enough" money that we lose sight of, and lack the time to live, the life to which God has called us. Mihaly Csikszentmihalyi captures the essence of the problem: "Caught in the treadmill of social controls, that person keeps reaching for a prize that always dissolves in his hands." The result is that we become "dependent on a social system that exploits our energies for its own purposes."[9] And contemplative Thomas Merton, in his struggle for a life of simplicity and self-denial, exclaims, "What a strange thing! In fulfilling myself, I had emptied myself. In grasping things, I had lost everything. In devouring pleasures and joys, I had found distress and anguish and fear."[10] Trapped on this hedonistic treadmill, we ignore the plight of the homeless, the mentally ill, the recently divorced church member, our neighbor's child with special needs, and others who are under-privileged and under-served.

In our pursuit of earthly accomplishments and material goods, our focus on God becomes obscured. Jesus warns, "For where your treasure is, there your heart will be also" (Matthew 6:21). Often, it takes a life crisis to jar us into realizing how twisted our lives have become. The path back to a God-centered life always begins with repentance of our offenses against God—of that which pits our wants against that which God knows we need. In God's grace we find forgiveness, and, yet again, take up our cross along the path of discipleship. Episcopal priest and author Barbara Cawthorne Crafton describes this as the "collision between our appetites and the needs of our souls." She reminds us that the "only way back to life (is) to set all our packages down and begin again, carrying with us what we really need."[11]

Jesus warns, "No one can serve two masters, for either he will hate the one and love the other, or he will be devoted to the one and despise the other. You cannot serve God and money" (Matthew 6:24). I have met attorneys, business leaders, accountants, and many other professionals who realize belatedly that the career they had chosen was not their true calling. These women and men want to follow their true call, yet feel trapped by the need to maintain the lifestyle to which they and their families have become accustomed. This is truly a spiritual dilemma, one in which they see themselves as imposters, attempting to fulfill their professional obligations only because they remained chained to their upscale lifestyle.

Empty of purpose and calling, their lives too often begin a downward spiral leading to problems with alcohol, extramarital affairs, sexual addiction, or other self-destructive behavior. Their struggle to maintain the facade exacts a high price from the very people whose needs they sought to meet through their high-paying jobs, and the social status that comes along it. Looking back, many would gladly have traded such achievements to avoid the pain of a failed marriage or destroyed career. A great tragedy is that many of these families would have supported their husbands, wives, fathers, and mothers, had they followed a different, healthier call to service.

All of us, at some point in our lives, will wake up one day and ask, "Is this all there is?" Csikszentmihalyi observes that when this realization sets in, people react in different ways. Some redouble their efforts to impress—they buy a prestigious car or a bigger home, grasp at more power, or adopt a glamorous lifestyle. Others, in an attempt to forestall further damage their choices have wrought, get plastic surgery, join a health club, or enroll in self-help courses. Some deny the problem, losing themselves in a dream world of alcohol or drugs. Others retire gracefully into the relative oblivion of a golf course, or take up residence in Sun City.[12] And, for some, it takes the reality of impending death before they realize that their possessions have no ultimate meaning.

Scripture provides us with another option. We can make choices that aren't based on monetary calculations. Recall the rich man who asked Jesus, "What must I do to inherit eternal life?" Jesus responded, "You lack one thing: go, sell all that you have and give to the poor, and you will have treasure in heaven; and come, follow Me" (Mark 10:17, 21). Jesus is not demanding that we live a life of deprivation. Rather, He is calling us to a life that is more fulfilling than that which the world has to offer, one in which success does not depend on social stature or material possessions. In fact, these often merely get in the way.

To live a life of significance means understanding that material possessions can be either an integral asset in our service to others or a barrier to strengthening our relationship with God. In themselves, money and material possessions are neither good nor bad. The difference is how we perceive their significance in the context of our Christian lives, and, out of that perception, how we use our resources. Paul instructed Timothy, "As for the rich in this present age, charge them not to be haughty, nor to set their hopes on the uncertainty of riches, but on God, who richly provides us with everything to enjoy" (1 Timothy 6:17). Rather, "They [we] are to do good, to be rich in good works, to be generous and ready to share, thus storing up treasure for themselves as a good foundation for the future, so that they may take hold of that which is truly life" (1 Timothy 6:18–19).

> To live a life of significance means understanding that material possessions can be either an integral asset in our service to others or a barrier to strengthening our relationship with God.

We can't have it both ways. If we do not control our resources, they will control us. In choosing to follow the call to worldly satisfaction, we choose *against* Christ's call to follow Him. A life of simplicity is a life of integrity, wherein we incorporate material goods as tools to enhance our vocational callings. Where the world might see climbing the corporate or political ladder as a legitimate life strategy, we see such priorities as a potential barrier to our call to serve.

The pursuit of possessions in order to achieve earthly success is, at base, a deception. We believe we won't be happy until we get what we want; yet getting what we want won't bring true satisfaction. We struggle to get more, in the blind trust that doing so will make us "worthy" in the eyes of others. We are like hamsters on the treadmill, running to "keep up," when, in reality, we are expending a lot of energy going nowhere. It is by calling to mind our Baptism that we are freed from this cycle of futility. Therein we discover our self-worth based on true riches—the forgiveness and peace purchased for us by Christ's sacrifice. This frees us for compassionate action. Rochelle Melander and Harold Eppley explain well,

> Because we no longer have to worry about our status in the realm of God—we are free to act boldly *for* the welfare of others. The "pressure" is off. The outcome has been decided. We don't have to worry that our actions or missteps will somehow lose us the keys to the kingdom. What we do with our lives says "thank you" to God; it's our gift back to God for all that God has done for us. We have been made free by God, and in that gracious state, we can use all that God has given us to act on behalf of those we meet each day.[13]

The truth is simple, but profound: In "losing" ourselves for the sake of this Gospel, we gain our souls. We live now out of the faith that God's action on our behalf changes all the rules. As our estimation of ourselves based on worldly values diminishes, so does our need for material possessions. We become fit vehicles for the Holy Spirit's work of reshaping our lives so that we might reshape the world.

From my perspective, we can take three definite, measurable steps toward this kind of life. First, take yet another honest inventory of your current life. Which possessions are you unduly attached to—your professional role, your house, physical beauty, brand-name clothes, your automobile, or the size of your paycheck? Ask, "If I were to lose any of these tomorrow, would I feel less a child of God?" If the answer is *yes* (and, in honesty, we all will say yes, at times), it is a clear indication that we must go back to square one to recommit to our rituals. We established these for the very purpose of aligning our values with God's.

Now, list any earthly possessions that you believe have the potential to become an idol—to dislodge God as the object of your deepest devotion:

1. _____

2. _____

3. _____

4. _____

5. _____

Are any of your attachments impeding your ability to serve your family? Was your choice of a college major driven solely by the desire for prestige or earning power? Does your need for status or wealth prevent you from pursuing the calling that God has created uniquely for you?

The second step is to create and implement rituals by which you can regain control of your material possessions and position, and use them to God's advantage. For Laurie and me, it means committing to a lifestyle that does not consume more than half of our annual income. We have made a conscious decision to not trade up to a larger home in a "nicer" neighborhood. We drive our cars until the odometer rolls over to the sixth digit. We avoid buying expensive clothing. This way of life allows us to make a tithe the beginning point of our giving to our congregation, Lutheran Social Services, and other worthwhile charities. We are able to save properly for our retirement and for Sydney's future. We can afford the tuition for Sydney to attend a Christian school. When new career opportunities come our way, we can evaluate them based not on our need for more money but on whether we believe it is the best move for our family in light of our service to God.

List five rituals that you can implement in order to assist you in leading a life of simplicity.

1. _____

2. _____

3. _____

4. _____

5. _____

The third step is to list how you can utilize your possessions to serve others: your used clothing for a homeless family; your car to drive a disabled woman to the doctor; your time to visit residents in the nursing home; your money to increase your weekly offering; or your position to urge those within your "constellation" of dots to support a worthy cause.

1. _____

2. _____

3. _____

4. _____

5. _____

Such selfless action results when we look to God and thus remain anchored to our true self—that which God re-created in Christ. If we hang on to our possessions, we will be condemned to a life of continual striving, one in which the brass ring remains tantalizingly out of reach.

Eckhart Tolle states that we say, "I don't have enough yet," by which the ego really means, "I am not enough yet."[14] When I as a Christian say, "I don't have enough yet," what I am really saying is that I have lost sight of God as center of my life; I acknowledge that I am not living a life of significance. Each of us, at some point, will find ourselves caught on the horns of this spiritual dilemma. The only way to become unhooked is by returning to the foot of the cross. There we are forgiven, and there the Spirit reorients our priorities so that we can joyfully use our assets to serve those God have placed in our path.

Our future need not be determined by uncaring, outside societal forces. Instead, the life of simplicity, of discipleship, unleashes us from society's paradigm of success, and the more *truly* satisfied we are. We find rest from chronic dissatisfaction. We discover *the peace that transcends all understanding*.

13
THE EIGHTH STRATEGY

CARING FOR OURSELVES

Do you not know that your body is a temple of the
Holy Spirit within you, whom you have from God?
You are not your own, for you were bought with a
price. So glorify God in your body.
—1 Corinthians 6:19–20

Caring for ourselves is a vital element in our eight-part strategy to live
a life of significance. By the creative use of rituals we can enhance our
physical, emotional, and spiritual well-being, and effectively fulfill our
vocational callings at work, home, community, and congregation. Self-

care is a way to live out our re-created selves, and by which we model responsible and appropriate self-love for those around us. In so doing, we increase our chances for a longer and healthier life. St. Paul exhorts:

> I appeal to you therefore, brothers, by the mercies of God, to present your bodies as a living sacrifice, holy and acceptable to God, which is your spiritual worship. Do not be conformed to this world, but be transformed by the renewal of your mind, that by testing you may discern what is the will of God, what is good and acceptable and perfect. (Romans 12:1–2)

Martin Luther develops this line of thought by linking care for ourselves with our care for others:

> The Christian should be guided by this one thing alone that he may serve and benefit others in all that he does, considering nothing except the need and the advantage of his neighbor. . . . This is what makes caring for the body a Christian work, that through its health and comfort we may be able to work, to acquire and lay by funds with which to aid those who are in need, that in this way the stronger member may serve the weaker. . . . This is a truly Christian life. Here faith is active in love.[1]

It is never too late to embark on—or to better—our path toward wellness. I am not talking merely about joining a fitness club or cramming a couples retreat into a "free" weekend (though those may be part of the equation). Such a piecemeal approach is ego-driven, and ends up being a fruitless search for the proverbial fountain of youth. True wellness is *shalom*—the harmony of body, mind, and spirit that God intended for us at creation. Such wholeness enables us to be good stewards of who we are and what we own in order to serve others.

A balanced lifestyle, therefore, is not just a "good idea" in theory; empirical evidence shows that by serving others, our own well-being is enhanced.[2] In other words, by definition, we can realize the harmony God intended for us only when we are in relationship with God and with others. Toward that end, the Ten Commandments provide both the privilege and responsibility for God-pleasing behavior toward all of God's creation—including ourselves! When we keep the Commandments, they in turn "keep" us. When we serve others, our own health is positively impacted.

The journey toward wholeness is multi-dimensional—it is one that incorporates intention and activity in our physical, emotional, and spiritual lives. And it is not always easy, for the temptation is for us to carve out a single, narrow path. As an aid to keep us focused, I offer three specific strategies:

1. Strengthen our relationship with God.

2. Implement rituals that include regular exercise, healthy eating, good habits, and availing ourselves of proper services for medical and psychological health.

3. Focus on the *doing* and *being* aspect of our lives.

Garth Ludwig eloquently describes the correlation between the health of our soul and the health of our body:

> The life of the spirit is the foundationstone of our human identity and integrates all other aspects of our personhood in the purposiveness of living. If the spirit is alienated from God, this is bound to have consequences in a person's character as well as in a person's health. Jesus confirmed the truth of this process when He said, "If then the light within you is darkness, how great is that darkness" (Matt. 6:23).[3]

As always, we begin with our relationship with God, in which we strive to be outward-focused. We live each day as saint and sinner, both broken and made whole, to be effective tools for God's work. And we establish rituals to help us honor our commitment to treat our bodies as "holy" temples. These include practices that provide for rest, renewal, and refreshment. We set aside time to worship God, to recharge our batteries, to reconnect with family and friends. These periods of reflection help us to discern God's will—which priorities and pursuits is He calling us to keep, and what are those we should let go? Gordon MacDonald draws an important distinction between *rest* and *leisure*. Leisure implies some form of amusement that provides momentary relief for our bodies, but not rest for our souls. True rest, says MacDonald, results when we pause in our activities to reflect on the truths and commitments by which we are living. He urges us to ask:

1. What does my work mean?

2. For whom did I do this work?

3. How well was the work done?

4. By what truth did I make my various commitments?

5. By what truth did I invest my resources and my time?[4]

MacDonald reminds us that "We do not rest because our work is done; we rest because God commanded it and created us to have a need for it."[5] We take advantage of this time to assess whether we are devoting our lives toward that which is significant and meaningful.

To avoid being overwhelmed by this task, we categorize the various aspects of our lives into modes of *being* or *doing*. Both are valuable. Both are necessary. The challenge is to be aware of which mode we are living in any given moment. The gift of our *being with* God enables our *doing for* others with compassion. Roy Oswald says that there are positive and negative traits in what he calls this "doing-being" tension. Below is an adaptation of Oswald's chart.[6]

Doing: Positives	Being: Positives
Helping a friend with homework	Prayer, Bible study, taking Communion
Exploring new ways to serve others	Rest, revitalization, and spiritual renewal
Volunteering at your daughter's school	Gaining perspective
Counseling a family member or friend	Acknowledging one's limitations
Being strong for others	Accepting oneself
Witnessing to others	Being grounded through words and actions
Doing: Negatives	**Being: Negatives**
Burnout	Spiritual narcissism
Overextending oneself	Becoming over-focused on one's self
Neglecting one's own needs	Isolation
Neglecting friends and family	Navel gazing
Becoming cynical	Loss of concern for others
Being overwhelmed by problems	Loss of sense of mission
Becoming exhausted and humorless	Hypochondria
Physical or emotional illness	Becoming part of the "me" generation
Being at one's worst	Excessive self-absorption

As you look at this chart, determine the quadrant in which you would locate your life at this moment. (My hope is that, by practicing the principles in this book, you find yourself in the upper right-hand quadrant.) In reality, all of us at times find ourselves trapped in one of the two lower quadrants. Being stuck in the *negative doing* quadrant is a sure sign that life has become merely a series of activities that leave us drained. It is a visual reminder for us to cease our *doing* and focus on those rituals that allow us to enjoy *being* with God. In the same way, finding ourselves in the *negative being* quadrant indicates that our ego is driving our lives. It is a call for us to assess whether we are in control of our material possessions or whether they are controlling us. We seek opportunities to be of service to others as we focus on moving back to the *positive doing* quadrant.

Take another look at the *Doing—Being* Chart. What three activities or rituals can you think of that will help you move from those times when you find yourself trapped in the *negative doing* quadrant to the *positive being* quadrant:

1. _____

2. _____

3. _____

Now, list three activities or rituals that you have found useful to help move you from the *negative being* quadrant to the *positive doing* quadrant.

1. _____

2. _____

3. _____

The chart places in bold relief the positive and negative aspects of the being/doing tension that characterizes our lives. Indeed, our physical and emotional health may suffer for a time when we focus on serving others. We might spend the night in a hospital with someone who is sick or dying; grieve with a family that has lost a child; or volunteer to help those who have lost everything in a natural disaster. We may even sacrifice our life in service to our country. By these actions we are, as Paul says, literally offering our bodies as "living sacrifices," being the hands and feet of God on earth.

Dietrich Bonhoeffer calls this "costly grace." Abigail Rian Evans describes it as "becoming broken so that others may become whole." Roland Miller reminds us that "Christ the Healer did not only suffer as he healed: he suffered in order to heal."[7] We become broken because that is what God calls us to do. As Bonhoeffer states, "To endure the cross is not a tragedy; it is the suffering which is the fruit of an exclusive allegiance to Jesus Christ."[8] We become broken so that others may become well. And by our brokenness we witness to the unique qualities of Christian discipleship.

Keeping God at the center of our hearts, incorporating rituals that help us focus on what is truly important, honestly telling our story, and intentionally living a life of simplicity provide us with the tools to blend the positive aspects of our *being* and our *doing* as we care for ourselves and live out our lives of worship and service.

PART THREE

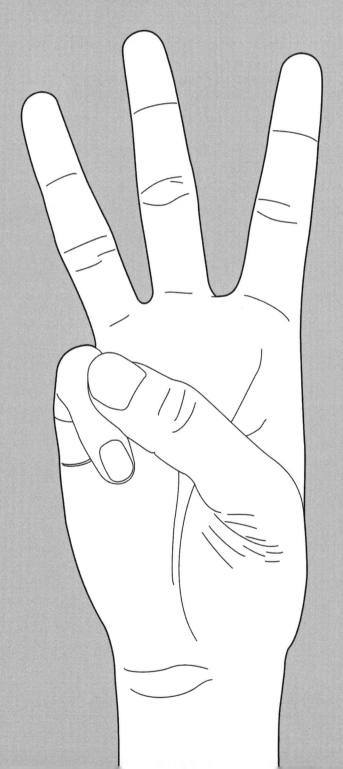

Living Out Our Calling

There is nothing better for them than to be joyful
and to do good as long as they live; also that
everyone should eat and drink and take pleasure
in all his toil—this is God's gift to man.
—Ecclesiastes 3:12–13

We continue our quest to live a life of significance by exploring the four primary vocations to which God calls us—family, work, community, and congregation. When we integrate each into the eight strategies previously outlined, the sum becomes greater than its parts. In the process, we begin to comprehend the words of C. S. Lewis: "To follow the vocation does not mean happiness; but once it has been heard, there is no happiness for those who do not follow."[1] Instead of the loneliness that accompanies an ego-driven attempt to be what *we* want to be, we discover the peace that accompanies our path to become who God calls us to be.

We will explore in the following chapters two areas not normally characterized as "callings"—those of suffering and of dying. Some might argue that these are not vocations in the truest sense but are rather the consequences of sin, and therefore experiences that must merely be endured. That is true, but it is incomplete insofar as it goes. A distinctive trait of Christian discipleship is that our suffering is not without purpose. It is one of the many paradoxes of our faith that suffering and death are both the result of sin, and yet are the avenues by which God sculpts us into caring individuals, after the fashion of Christ, created to serve and not to be served. In fact, it is not too bold to say that it is how we embrace our suffering, and ultimately, anticipate our dying, that determines the significance of the life we lead.

Our suffering is not without purpose.

The thoughts and suggestions I propose here are intended to be instructive, not prescriptive. The purpose is to provide a context and a framework for our daily actions that is both natural and strategic. Just as each of us bears a unique fingerprint, so each has a unique calling to serve, to embrace the words of the prophet Micah to live a life that is just, merciful, and humble (Micah 6:8).

14

SERVING OUR FAMILY

But as for me and my house,
we will serve the LORD.
—Joshua 24:15

t is a basic truth that not all families are the same, and that we fulfill different roles, according to our place in the design of our families. Not all of us are parents. Some are grandparents; others will never marry or have children. We are aunts, uncles, cousins, nephews, nieces, children, and grandchildren. We live with our adopted parents or our birth families. And the nature of our relationships with one another may not follow traditional lines. A teenager may be more likely to listen to her "cool" aunt, or an older cousin, than to her own father. A grandparent may be in a position to positively impact a grandchild's life in ways that the parents may not. Our family calling differs depending on which "mask" we are asked to wear. While, in some contexts, mask-wearing is seen as a negative and artificial metaphor, I mean it here as a way to express in a positive way the reality of our various roles. For example, I play the primary roles of spouse, father, son, son-in-law, brother, and uncle; each of these I call a mask. My responsibility in each role is complicated by the fact that some family members live out of state, some closer to home and have significant health issues, and several nephews and nieces rely on us for guidance and support. Most important, my spouse needs my love, support, and friendship, and my daughter needs an engaged father and role model. Your family responsibilities are likely as complex, and perhaps more so. Changes in society and culture have resulted in a variety of blended family structures. Each is an opportunity to shape our care to meet the specific situation in which we find ourselves.

On some level we may understand that serving our family is our first priority. But the reality is that we often give it too little attention, and always with unhealthy consequences. Sociologist Arlie Hocschild warns, "For all the talk about the importance of children, the cultural climate has become subtly less hospitable to parents who put children first. This is not because parents love children less, but because a 'job culture' has expanded at the expense of a 'family culture.' "[1] Money is a major driver behind this shift, as many families feel the pressure to have two paychecks to cover mortgages, taxes, groceries, college tuition, health care, and 401K plans.

Another compounding factor is the way home and work environments have evolved, the demands of the latter engulfing our good intention to keep the former as our main priority. We feel the need to produce overlapping daily, monthly, quarterly, and yearly outcomes at work, or else suffer the consequences of demotion, or even be without a job. We are surrounded by the symbols of material success, and face the endless challenge to keep up with our peers. To do so, we must expend the most energy in our professional roles, where we strive to perform well and behave our best, and hope that we will be rewarded for our efforts. All this takes a serious toll at home, where we frequently come through the door at the end of the day physically and emotionally exhausted. Unlike the atmosphere at work, at home there is often no sense of task completion, or ability to quantify the nature of relationships. Add to this the technological distractions of texting, television, and the looming expectations of a 24/7 work cycle, and it becomes difficult, at best, to spend quantity and quality time with our loved ones.[2]

These contradictory dynamics don't make our calling to serve our family any less important. The following data is a sobering reminder for me of what reality might look like in my family were I not to play an active role in Sydney's life:

- In a home where the father is absent, a teenage girl is three times more likely to engage in sexual relations by the time she is 15 years old;

- Teens in homes where the father is absent are at greater risk for illegal drug use;

- Children in father-absent homes have a higher rate of asthma, anxiety, or depression, and behavioral problems.[3]

I could not entertain a call to any vocation or opportunity, no matter how tempting, if it would be in competition with my vocation as father to our daughter and would expose her to these risks. We must remain constantly aware that we are swimming upstream against societal and professional pressures as we strive to fulfill our family calling.

Serving our family well does not have to be a zero sum game *vis-à-vis* other vocations. A sick child, an elderly parent, an afternoon soccer match, a parent-teacher conference all demand time that we would otherwise probably spend at work. But, as we have seen repeatedly thus far, tending to one area of our lives—in this case, our family—positively impacts all other areas. Research demonstrates that organizational leaders who enjoy solid, healthy relationships and a balanced family life are more likely to be more creative and successful in the workplace.[4] It is also empirically demonstrable that the more we focus outward, the healthier we are.[5]

Chances are that most of you reading this book are or will become married. Through our marriage we are united and "become one flesh" (Genesis 2:24). The old adage is true: marriage takes work. We must be proactive in keeping this "oneness" God-pleasing, willing to give all of ourselves—body, mind, and spirit—to our partner for the joy of mutual blessing. On an emotional level, we share our thoughts, needs, burdens, fears, dreams, weaknesses, and hopes. Spiritually, we join hands in prayer, kneel at the Lord's Table regularly, forgive and encourage each other, and promise to love and persevere. Physically, we enrich each other when we take part in activities that enhance our bodies and help us appreciate each other in our love-making—the most tender expression of intimacy. In a godly marriage, husband and wife follow God's will for them, set aside ego, accept each other for who they are (warts and all), and rejoice that their spouse is a precious child of God. Then we are well positioned for a life of service to each other.

Laurie and I believe that we can better fulfill our individual callings when we function as a partnership. The state of our family's health is directly related to how effective we are in our goal to live a life of significance. Our partnership enhances my ability to serve the clients of Lutheran Social Services; when work is stressful, Laurie helps keeps me balanced. Similarly, Laurie feels supported in her life when I encourage and support the activities and relationships by which she strives to lead a life of significance. We understand each other's strengths and weaknesses, and we draw upon each other's care. The three of us have come to appreciate how our individual threads, when woven together, form a strong setting that holds us up and enables us to serve others.

Martin Luther suggested that anyone wanting to understand the meaning of self-sacrifice should marry and have children.[6] This statement hit home for Laurie and me when Sydney was born. Suddenly, our lives were turned upside down. We had no choice but to make sure that she was cared for around the clock. No longer did we have the luxury of sleeping in on weekends, or dropping everything to go on an unplanned romantic vacation. We chose to make Sydney the focus of our family life. For me, the question was no longer, "What do I want to do?" but, "How can I best serve my family?" We voluntarily (albeit, not always easily) stepped away from our selfish egos, diminished our demands, and strived instead for what we felt was best for our entire family. Thereby we began to grasp

Jesus' daunting words, "If anyone would come after Me, let him deny himself and take up his cross and follow Me" (Mark 8:34).

In our role as father or mother we are also called to wear the "mask" of God. Luther, with characteristic earthiness, says that when we change the dirty diapers of our child, we should imagine we are holding the baby Jesus in our hands, since what we are doing is truly angel's work.[7] Wearing the "mask" of God in this fashion keeps us from seeing our familial obligations—being the carpool mom, doing the drudgery of laundry, or mowing the lawn—as burdensome or as a loss of personal freedom. In the process, we become less "me-centric," and more "God-centric." We ask, "How does God want me to serve my family today?" "Why has God placed me in this particular role, at this specific time, in this exact location?"

Also helpful in our move from an inward to an outward perspective in our family role is the distinction between what has been identified as *form-based* and *formless* attention. Form-based attention encompasses our typical parental roles of *doing* and *evaluating*: Eat your vegetables. Get your Spanish grade up. Don't forget to take the trash out. While form-based attention is necessary, it is not the most important. Formless attention is even more vital. At its simplest, it can be described as being completely present *in the moment*. It is the recognition that our child, our parent, our spouse, are valued for who they are, that nothing else is as important as they are at that particular moment. It is the realization that, in that moment, our love is unconditional, our attention is undivided, and that we are fully present in the room with them, and that they are precious children of God.[8] When we are completely present, our own needs diminish, and we become attuned to the needs of others.

When we are completely present, our own needs diminish, and we become attuned to the needs of others.

The Book of Proverbs instructs, "Train up a child in the way he should go; even when he is old he will not depart from it" (22:6). As adults, it is our responsibility to help young people discover and live out God's plan and purpose. This encompasses their faith life, career plans, family interactions, community involvement, and social network. We accomplish this through both form-based and formless attention. Children want and need us to set boundaries and provide instruction. These are expressions of form-based attention. Even more, they crave the gift of formless attention—that of being recognized and valued for who they are apart from what they do or our evaluation of their behavior. This deepens our relationships, changes the way we interact, and opens up the path for us to be positive influences. When I focus on providing formless attention, I notice my habits change. Dinner in our home has become off-limits for television, texting, and phone calls. We plan occasional weekend trips when we can practice formless attention with one another. Then we have no choice but to play games, engage in conversation, and explore new sites—all priceless opportunities to laugh, cry, and pray together.

Fulfilling our family vocation extends beyond our flesh-and-blood relations. Many families embrace the opportunity to serve as a foster family or to adopt a child. Worldwide there are a staggering 148 million orphans. In the United States, 127,000 children over the age of eight are languishing in foster care, considered "unadoptable."[9] There are countless ways we can fulfill the biblical injunction to care for the orphan (Isaiah 1:16–17), open our home to a child in need, and support organizations that serve children at risk.

The story of Irene and Billy Clements is exemplary. Christmastime, nearly a decade ago, the couple wondered how they could best meet the various needs of their family, which included adopted and foster children, as well as their birth children. A few days before, Irene had received an unexpected call from the Salvation Army, asking if they would be willing to take in 13-year-old Beverly so she wouldn't have to spend the holidays alone in the shelter. Thinking back, Irene remembers that the week ahead was already jammed with meeting the needs of their family, overnight guests, and an assortment of other folks. Nevertheless, she reluctantly agreed. At week's end, Irene recalls, she felt guilty for not having devoted more time to Beverly. The adolescent had been somewhat overlooked amidst the holiday excitement. Some ten years later, Irene received a call—from

Beverly! She wondered if Irene remembered her, then nervously went on to ask if she might come over to introduce her fiancé to them. Although surprised by the request, Irene naturally assented. During their visit, Beverly told Billy and Irene that the one week she had spent in their home was the only time in her life she felt she was a "member" of a functional, Christian family. Upon their engagement, Beverly told her fiancé she was committed to creating the same kind of healthy family dynamic she experienced that Christmas a decade ago. Wearing the masks of God, Irene and Billy made a lasting impact on this impressionable young girl, and in the process may have helped break a multigenerational cycle of violence, abuse, and resulting poverty.

There is great potential for us to serve as models for families around us. As managers, we can create an organizational culture that encourages a balanced lifestyle. We can serve as Big Brothers or Big Sisters, or volunteer in such organizations like Boys and Girls Clubs of America. We can be active participants in our congregation's marriage classes, Sunday School, youth, and singles groups. The doors of opportunity are many. All that remains is for us to step through.

The Eight Strategies

Because the call to serve our families is wide-ranging, and can sometimes feel out of control, it is useful to have help in shaping that role. The Eight Strategies provide a framework that helps keep the task manageable. Primary in this arena, as in all areas of life, is the need to keep God at the center. This is easier said than done. Even in "model" families, life, in all its messiness, happens: romantic love ebbs and flows; necessity forces us to compromise in order to keep the peace; raging hormones contribute to teenage angst. Bills, illness, unemployment, travel, overtime, and caring for a sick parent add stress to any family. Such challenges scream for our attention and leave us little time or energy to tend to our spiritual life. We may at times feel miles away from fulfilling Jesus' command, "You shall love the Lord your God with all your heart and with all your soul and with all your strength and with all your mind" (Luke 10:27). It takes everything we have to keep from throwing up our hands and yelling, "I give up!" When we reach this point, it is a sure sign that we are trying to play God, rather than allowing God to uphold us. It is in these times of desperation that Jesus invites us to rest in Him, to "let go and let God," to experience the "love, joy, peace, patience, kindness, goodness, faithfulness, gentleness, [and] self-control" (Galatians 5:22–23), that are the fruit of the Spirit.

Postmodern society is making it increasingly difficult for us to order our lives according to God's expectations. William Placher describes the time in which we live as most closely resembling that of the Early Church. Those who called themselves Christians were a minority, albeit a rapidly growing one. They were often forced to disassociate from their family, endure insufferable hardships, and meet in secret in order to avoid being persecuted for their beliefs. Many scholars propose that today we have come full circle. In Europe, and in many parts of the United States, openly practicing the Christian faith is less and less considered "normal." Placher explains:

> The values of our culture seem to have so much to do with acquiring the lifestyles of the rich and famous. Advertising surrounds us with images of sexual pleasure and material wealth. "What is God calling me to do?" or, "How can I pick up my cross and follow Jesus?"—these seem even stranger questions. Trying to live as a Christian pushes upstream against the dominant values around us.[10]

In this culture, it is our calling to be *counter*cultural, to live our faith "out loud," to let others see our beliefs in action—in other words, to live a life of significance. Young people need to observe us going to church, praying at home and in public, and engaging in conversations about the importance of serving others. To paraphrase Luther, we must learn to be apostles to our children.[11]

An older woman recently described to me how this point became crystal clear to her, as she talked about the differences and similarities between her and her sisters. All three were raised in the same home. Yet, the children and grandchildren of only one sister seemed to be living "successful" lives—they were still in their first marriage, enjoyed healthy relationships with their friends, and held responsible jobs. Of the three sisters, it was this one who, along with her husband, practiced their Baptist faith regularly and made sure their children were involved in the life of their church. When this sister's two daughters left home, they took with them a model for their own life choices, including whom they married and how to instill Christlike values in their children. The other sisters, while they professed to be Christian, had not practiced those things that would help ensure their own children would enjoy the blessings of a Christ-filled home.

In this culture, it is our calling to be countercultural, to live our faith 'out loud,' to let others see our beliefs in action—in other words, to live a life of significance.

The influence that family has on our own lives cannot be overstated. Look again at the dot-constellation you diagrammed in the Second Strategy on p. 42. The lines connecting you to past and future generations represent pathways by which your parents and grandparents have influenced you, and how you, in turn, are influencing those after you. At Lutheran Social Services, I have seen firsthand the impact that abuse, addiction, neglect, and divorce has across generations. As I look at my own constellation of dots, I am reminded of how blessed I am for ancestors that, while not perfect, did their best to instill Christian values and model a life of discipleship. Laurie and I take seriously the part we play in passing on this torch to Sydney, knowing full well the negative ramifications on future generations if we fail in this mission.

Seeing the lines that connect us with our forbears also means we see how we can learn from their mistakes. If there is a history of alcoholism in our family, we can be especially watchful for signs of addictive behavior in our children or ourselves. If there is a history of abuse, we can access family counseling to help break the cycle. If our parents did not affiliate with a congregation, we can start a new tradition of churchgoing. Once we see that we have choices, we have the responsibility to choose those actions and behaviors that will best serve our children and grandchildren.

Incorporating rituals into our family life is fundamental to living a life of significance. Jesus provided us with the ultimate "ritual" when He said, "So whatever you wish that others would do to you, do also to them, for this is the Law and the Prophets" (Matthew 7:12). It is human for us to want to be loved, to be served, to be respected and valued by our family members. Our conscience reminds us also of our responsibility to give the same to our family. In this reciprocal "dance," we experience the beautiful give-and-take nature of Jesus' words. Shower your spouse with compliments and attention, and likely as not, you will reap the benefit of similar affection. Behave like an adult with your children—no slamming of doors or useless yelling—and, in turn, their respectful demeanor may surprise you. If you are struggling to forgive a friend who has slighted you, treat him or her with love. If you want your child to listen to your advice, give them your undivided attention when they are speaking.

Whatever you wish that others would do to you, do also to them. (Matthew 7:12)

We can gauge how well (or how poorly) we are fulfilling our family roles by asking ourselves the hard questions: Have I spent enough time with my niece, who values my guidance? Have I focused sufficient attention on Laurie to make sure that her needs are met? When was the last time I called, e-mailed, or visited my sister? My parents? What does my teenage daughter need from her father this week? This evening? The following exercise will help us identify the gaps between our actions and the needs of our family. There are not enough hours in the day to satisfy all needs, and we would burn out trying. Here is a chart to help us identify and draw boundaries around our family interactions:

Family Member	Sufficient Attention?	Plan to Remedy the Gap
Spouse	No	• Block out 45 minutes of uninterrupted time each evening
Children (List separately)	No	• Purchase tickets to upcoming game/play • Share a hobby • Help with homework
Grandparents	No	• Take them to dinner once a month • Go visit them next weekend
Parents	No	• Call every Saturday • Drop them a note saying how much you appreciate them
Siblings (List separately)	No	• Have regular contact via phone, e-mail, or Facebook • Plan to visit during summer vacation
Grandchildren (List separately)	No	• Monthly sleepover • Plan play dates • Let them know you are praying for them via text messages
In-laws	No	• Include on a vacation • Help with home maintenance • Go out to eat after church

Complete the following list now, either for yourself, with your spouse, or as a family. Use extra sheets if necessary.

Family Member	Sufficient Attention?	Plan to Remedy the Gap
Spouse	No	
Children (List separately)	No	
Grandparents	No	
Parents	No	
Siblings (List separately)	No	
Grandchildren (List separately)	No	
In-laws	No	

Our habits, both bad and good, become our lives, and often, our children's lives. A gentleman once commented sadly to me, "When I spend time with my grown son, all I see in him are my weaknesses." What habits or traits do you want to pass on—a fiery temper, a problem with alcohol, being an absent parent? Or do you want to pass on the ritual of a kiss when you walk out the door in the morning and return at night, saying "I love you" before going to bed; weekend visits to the bookstore with your son, or a semi-annual intergenerational family gathering? Even performing household chores, as insignificant as they may seem, can have a long-lasting impact on our children. Research published in the *American Journal of Sociology* studied 506 couples in the United States. Researchers found that, after controlling for other factors, the more that men participated in domestic chores, the more stable their marriage was. Another study of 3,000 adults revealed similar results. Those participants who performed household chores as a child were much more likely to engage in volunteer roles or perform community work as adults.[12]

> ## Our habits, both bad and good, become our lives, and often, our children's lives.

Fulfilling our family roles involves asking certain questions that demand honesty. For what purpose did God place me in my family? Will my current life, my "story," allow me to fulfill this purpose? Is the time and form of attention I am committing to my family sufficient? If my parents died today, would I feel at peace with the relationship we had? Are my health habits sufficient to enable me to enjoy my grandchildren? As you do an honest assessment of the mental picture you have painted, look for areas where you are especially vulnerable to "blind spots"—those areas where you may have white-washed your responses or minimized their negative impact.

The next step is to take action, to create rituals, to help transform your story into that which you believe God has created uniquely for you. This kind of self-reflection may touch areas of your life that you would just as soon leave alone. Don't let that dissuade you, for, in order to change, one must be willing to entertain new ways of doing things.

Take time now to briefly summarize the "story line" of one facet of your family story you would like to change. Then write what actions or rituals you will implement to bring about that transformation.

Story Line: _____

_____

Rituals: _____

_____

Using the framework of the two curves, we can conceptualize our family life both here and now, as well as in the future. We can help our children appreciate how the words and actions (rituals) we create today have positive consequences down the road. For example, your list might include such activities as volunteering at the hospital, going on a mission trip, or rescuing a stray dog. We can gently challenge our children by asking if they helped a classmate with homework, included a new student in their lunchtime conversation, or prayed for a stressed-out teacher.

It also falls to us as parents to educate our children about the realities that await them once they are out of school. What is needed at this point in their lives that will prepare them in their future work as an engineer, firefighter, musician, or cook? The daily media bombardment glamorizes celebrities and athletes, and exploits people and situations to make "reality" television scenarios, which can lead to the false belief that success will land on our children's doorstep without the need to sacrifice, study, or practice. Immersed in this cultural fiction, today's youth often relegate the stories of the toil and disappointments that their parents met on the path to adulthood as the "old days."

To function as mentors for our children as they plot their path along the second curve demands that we assess our own priorities. We can advertently fall into the trap of measuring their success against the yardstick of modern society. In encouraging them (with good intention) to pursue a career that will provide a "comfortable" living, we may be discouraging them from following their true calling. By pushing them toward enrolling in a prestigious university, we might be steering them away from a Christian college that could lay a firmer groundwork for a career. Do we ignore signals that they might not want to pursue formal education after high school, and support them instead to seek out a trade apprenticeship? Do we subtly downplay the fact that they may feel a call to ministry, in favor of encouraging them toward a better-paying job? To overlay our own insecurities onto their impressionable lives detracts from a life of significance for them, and for us.

Whatever path they choose, they—and we—live both in the kingdom of the world and the kingdom of the Church. We are to "seek first the kingdom of God" (Matthew 6:33) while, at the same time, learning to "be wise as serpents and as innocent as doves" (Matthew 10:16). There is a distinction between a corporate strategy that emphasizes fairness for all and one that manipulates its employees for the purpose of enhancing the "bottom line." To walk successfully in both kingdoms is to recognize that quality of life is defined not by what we do but by who we are as re-created in Christ.

Let me return to the idea of *flow*, as defined earlier by Mihaly Csikszentmihalyi. We might, applying a Christian perspective to the concept, talk about the "flow" of our baptismal waters. The relationship that God established with us at that time carries within it the capacity for us and our children to enjoy all of life with gracious ease. Csikszentmihalyi notes that "the family context that provides [for children] an ideal training for enjoying life has five characteristics":

1. **Clarity**—when teenagers feel they know what their parents expect from them, and goals and feedback within the family are unambiguous.

2. **Centering**—when children sense that their parents take an interest in their current lives, rather than being preoccupied with thoughts of their future success.

3. **Choice**—when children feel they have a variety of decisions and possibilities from which to choose—including that of breaking parental rules—as long as they are prepared to face the consequences.

4. **Commitment**—when an atmosphere of trust allows a child to set aside the shield of his defenses, and pursue his current interest unself-consciously.

5. **Challenge**—when parents provide for their children increasingly complex opportunities for action.[13]

Csikszentmihalyi notes that teenagers living in such an environment are "significantly more happy, satisfied, and strong in most life situations than their peers who did not have such a relationship."[14]

We can take Csikszentmihalyi's findings to the next level, so that, by holding up the Scriptures as the model, our children can see by our own example. Living a Christ-filled life of significance day by day is filled with choice, commitment, and challenge. Family members are made fit for the task by the Holy Spirit's strength and guidance. When our lives are not shaped by the example of Christ, our days become unmanageable and unrealistic

Scientists from the University of California, Los Angeles, researched the potential consequences when our lives are dominated by activities. Following thirty-two families over a four-year period, researchers found that those whose lives were over-programmed with work, after-school activities, and a myriad of other time-consuming events, lacked markedly time for play, conversation, courtesy, and intimacy. And when individual family members were at home at the same time, they were physically in the room only 16 percent of the time.[15] By simplifying our manic lives, we discover time for unstructured and spontaneous moments of attention, when we communicate how important the other is. We can celebrate our material blessings, rather than be overwhelmed by financial burden. Living a life of simplicity teaches our children to develop empathy and compassion for those who are less fortunate. In the words of Richard Foster, it allows us to remove them from the "ghettos of affluence," so that they can learn compassion and provide healing to the broken of the world.[16]

Whether we are aware of it or not, our youth are observing the decisions we make and the effects they have. By so doing, they see (though they may not be aware of it) the connection between our choices today and our lives down the road. Our example helps shape their decisions for responsible and moderate living here and now. They will face choices—spend weekend nights partying or choosing time for worship on Sunday mornings? Study or do drugs? Engage in promiscuous sexual activity or become involved in a God-pleasing relationship? Eat healthy or live on fast food? Use alcohol in moderation or engage in binge drinking? No matter our age, our family is counting on us to take care of our health. It is a given that we won't be able to live a life of significance if we suffer from smoking-related physical limitations or don't control our diabetes. It is not always easy to stick to a healthy lifestyle regimen, but the task becomes easier if we remember that our consistency and dedication to self-care also benefits those around us.

> Living a Christ-filled life of significance
> day by day is filled with choice,
> commitment, and challenge.

We can also—as individuals and as a family unit—locate where we are on the Doing—Being chart (see p. 107). Have we become overwhelmed by work, neglecting the needs of our family? What rituals do we need to implement to move back into the upper-right quadrant? Has our family become self-absorbed? What "positive doing" volunteer activities or rituals can we embrace that will help move us out of that negative quadrant? Are we quarreling more than usual? Have we distanced ourselves from our relationship with God? The goal is to create a family dynamic that incorporates a blend between *positive doing* and *positive being* quadrants. Thus, we maintain a balance so that our family is grounded in a life of care, service, and worship.

By our modeling, mentoring, and teaching, we can educate our children about caring for themselves and for others. None of us is perfect, however. There are times I realize that my life has been off balance—when, because of my self-absorption, I have neglected my family. I can identify with the character played by Jack Nicholson in the movie *As Good As It Gets*. In a rare moment of personal insight, he tells the caring and patient woman, played by Helen Hunt, "You make me want to be a better man." Laurie and Sydney, through their giving nature, kindness, and support, make me want to be a better husband and father. Their love inspires me to live a balanced life, focus on my relationship with God, be fully present for them when we are together, and serve them, as best I can, as Christ has served us.

At the end of the day, we are fortunate if we can say—and mean—it is family that matters most. Dietrich Bonhoeffer reflected on the importance of family. When imprisonment kept him from attending a relative's wedding, he wrote,

> Most people have forgotten nowadays what a home can mean, though some of us have come to realize it as never before. It is a kingdom of its own in the midst of the worlds, a haven of refuge amid the turmoil of our age, nay more, a sanctuary. It is not founded on the shifting sands of private and public life, but has a peace in God. For it is God who gave it its special meaning and dignity, its nature and privilege, its destiny and worth.[17]

15

SERVING OUR PROFESSION

Whatever you do, work heartily, as for the Lord
and not for men, knowing that from the Lord you
will receive the inheritance as your reward. You are
serving the Lord Christ. —**Colossians 3:23–24**

The Hebrew word *avodah* carries with it a double meaning: *worship* and *work*. In biblical usage, it means to revere, praise, be awed by, bow down to, and submit to the one true God. It also means to serve, labor, and work with all our heart. Together, the word paints, like a beautiful piece of art, the total balance of the work and worship cycle that mirrors God's creative pattern. Thereby, our professional calling is integrated into our faith; it becomes an attitude of the heart. This holds true regardless of the form our work takes: volunteer or paid; retired or active employed; part-time, full-time, or in between jobs; in school preparing for our career or considering a career change. Or, we may be like the widow in the Gospel of Luke, who served God by fasting and praying night and day in the temple (Luke 2:37). Our calling to our work, no matter what it is, is an integral aspect of our worship and service to our Lord.

We live in a time of job insecurity, corporate mergers, pressure to produce, mandatory overtime, and 24/7 schedules—all to meet our financial obligations and maintain our standing among peers. It is no wonder that we forget our job is, in essence, a calling to serve God. Societal values erase the biblical distinction between our Sundays and our Mondays, the separation of our work from our worship and recreation. Work is about crushing the competition, making a profit, climbing the corporate ladder. Work is merely a means by which we *achieve*. To see the real purpose of our work as *service*—to others and to God—is often considered quaint and naïve. Our pursuit of honest labor is not a matter of chasing the elusive pot of gold, but an opportunity to meld our faith into our labor.

Our pursuit of honest labor is not a matter of chasing the elusive pot of gold, but an opportunity to meld our faith into our labor.

Thus, we view work through a different lens that leads us to ask questions that get to the heart of the matter: Have I made a difference in someone's life today? Will my children respect me for how I do my work? What impact on society do I want to make today, this year, this decade? What are the ethical ramifications of my decisions at the office? How will these affect our customers and employees? Am I creating lasting value in the place where I am serving? Whether creating software, writing songs, building houses, or balancing the books, our work is an opportunity to serve God and others.

Martin Luther reminds us that God values all beneficial work equally:

> Every person surely has a calling. While attending to it he serves God. A king serves God when he is at pains to look after and govern his people. So do the mother of a household when she tends her baby, the father of a household when he gains a livelihood by working, and a pupil when he applies himself diligently to his studies. . . . Therefore, it is a great wisdom when a human being does what God commands and earnestly devotes himself to his vocation without taking into consideration what others are doing.[1]

Luther argues that there is no such thing as a lesser calling. All our work is holy. The janitor is not merely mopping floors. He serves on the front lines by protecting others from harmful bacteria and infections. A personal assistant isn't merely shuffling papers for his boss. He keeps the day running smoothly, so his boss can fulfill his obligations, and, in the process, enables his co-workers to do their jobs more efficiently.

How do you characterize your view toward your job? Stuck, with no place to go? Or completely engrossed and fulfilled? Most of us, depending on the day, vacillate between the two. Answering e-mail or refereeing disputes among employees take up valuable time. Cleaning up the break room after our inconsiderate co-workers; plowing the field before planting; taking the order of a gruff restaurant patron—all can become burdensome. Yet, through all, God is working. Once again we turn to Martin Luther:

> God's people please God even in the least and most trifling matters. For He will be working all things through you; He will milk the cow through you and perform the most servile duties through you, and all the greatest and least duties alike will be pleasing to Him.[2]

It is our privilege to seek out what God calls us to do. If we pursue a career merely to make more money or to satisfy our parents, we miss the joy of our true calling, and our days become drudgery. In the words of Antoine de Saint-Exupery, "the clay of which you were shaped has dried and hardened, and naught in you will ever awaken the sleeping musician, the poet, the astronomer that possibly inhabited you in the beginning."[3] If we are fortunate, we can see the signs warning that we are heading down this path. We may find we "need" a cocktail or two after work, argue with our spouse more than usual, or suffer a stress-related illness. These may be important indicators that our work is driving us rather than calling us. Gordon MacDonald describes how "driven" people often derive gratification solely from accomplishment. They become preoccupied by the symbols of achievement, tend to have less regard for integrity, are often highly competitive and abnormally busy, place little value on their spiritual lives, and may have an explosive anger. In contrast, MacDonald says that people who feel called to their work possess an uncanny strength from within. They know who they are, understand stewardship, have an unwavering sense of purpose, and practice unswerving commitment.[4] They have discovered the call by which they meld their God-given talents with the needs of the world.

It is our privilege to seek out what God calls us to do.

There is a danger in thinking that our current job is holding us back from doing what is really "important." We may feel restless, yet trapped, and believe that joy can be restored only by a change in our work or in location. For several years I toiled away in a law firm, pursuing legal action against corporations. I found the work tedious, often meaningless. It didn't take me long to discover this was not to be my lifelong work. In that process, however, I had missed the reality that God had placed me there for a reason. As I trace the line of God's leading backward, I can see that, despite my discontent, I was serving clients and learning valuable skills. God also used this time to teach me the craft of participating in the political process. It was during my time there that I helped care for a friend who suffered from severe depression. And, had I not been at the firm, I would not have been able to introduce a co-worker to my sister-in-law, which resulted in a long-lasting marriage.

I learned a valuable lesson through this experience. Luther reminds us not to automatically "think of changing (our) lot, but of changing (our) spirit of discontent."[5] Along the same lines, Albert Schweitzer states:

> Such persons wanted to dedicate themselves to larger tasks because those that lay nearest did not satisfy them. . . . Only a person who can find value in every sort of activity and devote himself to each one with full consciousness of duty, has the inward right to take as his object some extraordinary activity instead of that which falls naturally to his lot. Only someone who feels his preference to be a matter of course, not something out of the ordinary, and who has no thought of heroism, but just recognizes a duty undertaken with somber enthusiasm, is capable of becoming a spiritual adventurer such as the world needs. There are no heroes of action: only heroes of renunciation and suffering. Of such there are plenty. But few of them are known, and even these not to the crowd, but to the few.[6]

Recall the story of Zacchaeus, who, in his work as tax collector, cheated his own people (Luke 19:1–10). This man of short stature had climbed a tree to see a traveling preacher he had heard so much about. When Jesus spied Zacchaeus, He called him to come down, and insisted on eating supper at his home. The gracious call forever transformed the tax collector. Zacchaeus gave away half of his wealth to those in need and offered to provide restitution to anyone he had cheated. It is important to note that Zacchaeus continued in his job as tax collector, but he was called to do his job differently, to treat people fairly. Jesus' call enabled Zacchaeus to see his work as holy.

THE EIGHT STRATEGIES

Proverbs instructs, "Keep your heart with all vigilance, for from it flow the springs of life" (4:23). The Gospels tell us that Jesus spent time in solitude with His heavenly Father before He made important decisions or took action. This is our model as well. All of us experience the fatigue, stress, and frustrations that accompany our work. Sometimes, all that is required to "reset" is prayer, a good night's sleep, or a three-day weekend. Or the discontent may be on a deeper level, as we realize that God is no longer our primary focus in life. We pray less, complain more, become self-absorbed, and feel anxious and depressed. In these times of spiritual fatigue, we can return to the cross, where we find forgiveness and can begin again with our priorities now in line with God's will, and freed to work not for man but for the Lord (Colossians 3:23).

As we trace our collection of dots in relation to our profession, we see connections that may need realigning. In my role as CEO, I am expected to juggle the myriad of dots that are labeled employees, budgets, colleagues, attorneys, accountants, board members, stakeholders, clients, customers, media, politicians, and donors.

My tangled web may look something like this:

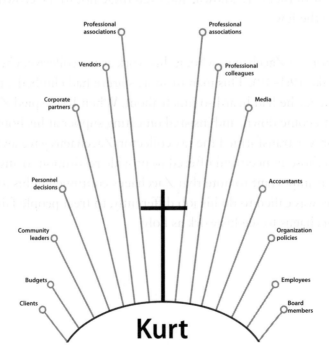

A student's web may look like this:

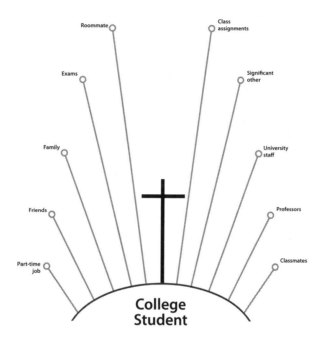

Create your diagram on page 138.

The diagram reveals the many opportunities we have to wear the "mask" of God as we serve others, in person-to-person encounters, and when these are taken collectively. The diagram above also reminds us of those times when our actions are irresponsible and hurtful, like when we gossip, disrespect a customer, improve our own status to the detriment of a colleague, or cheat on our expense account. We are comforted in knowing that we can ask forgiveness and, in faith, find strength to right our wrongs. By keeping the cross in the forefront of our professional lives we are constantly reminded of the spiritual significance of our everyday actions. This provides a framework for living out on Monday the grace and peace we heard about—and received at the Lord's Table—on Sunday. The Holy Spirit leads us as we shape our lives according to the values and ethics of

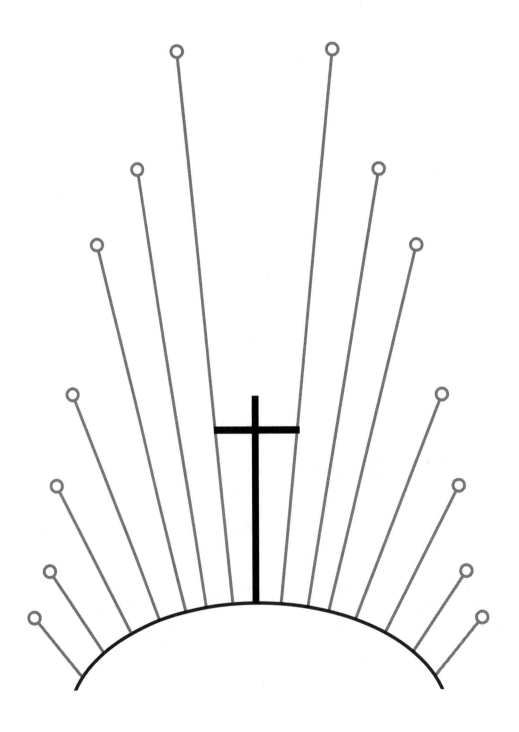

Christian discipleship. In so doing, even our most mundane and insignificant tasks become vital and challenging.

Rituals serve as a means to this end. To begin creating those rituals that will serve us, we ask ourselves important questions. Is the time and energy we expend in our professional vocation consistent with our deepest values? What is our God-given purpose in this vocation? Are we making the most of our abilities? Is there a disconnect between who we say we want to be and who we actually are? Are we taking advantage of the opportunities to be of service to others?

Next, we identify the gaps between who we are and who we want to be in our professional lives. Then, we outline and implement rituals to close these gaps. Perhaps we might take some continuing education to round out our skill sets. Maybe we can mentor someone who can benefit from our experience. Can we name at least one person every day we can go out of our way to serve? Is there a breakfast Bible study we can attend before we begin our workday?

Below are rituals I've identified:

- Serve as a mentor to our younger leaders.

- Lead my Austin-area staff in regular devotions.

- Have conversations randomly with employees and clients to discover how I can be of service to them.

- Make weekly worship with my family a priority over my professional obligations.

What will you commit to? Take time to list several rituals that will assist you in closing the gaps in your identity at work or at school—to help connect your Sundays to your Mondays.

Sundays	Mondays
1. _____ _____	1. _____ _____
2. _____ _____	2. _____ _____
3. _____ _____	3. _____ _____
4. _____ _____	4. _____ _____
5. _____ _____	5. _____ _____

We might view the call to our work as a story. Some of us are in the middle of the book, others are just stepping from the introduction to the first chapter, or perhaps busy rewriting paragraphs. And some are putting on paper the flourishes of their last chapter that brings to a conclusion a life of faithful service. But we are not the sole author. Throughout our lives, God is moving—sometimes obviously, sometimes mysteriously—in and out of the narrative that is our story. Holding our lives up to the mirror of God's Book and looking deep within ourselves, we ask whether there are sections that need editing—or total rewriting. Do we need to return to school? Should we simplify our lifestyle? Have we confused our *need* to achieve success with God's desire for us? Is our "driven-ness" leading us away from proper attention to family and to personal health?

Recently, a good friend was offered a partnership in a successful national consulting firm. He asked me to help him through the discernment process. To accept the offer would involve a five- to ten-year commitment. I began by asking:

- What is your ultimate purpose? Why did God place you here at this particular time and in this particular place? Is your current work helping you live out your faith journey? What unique talents has God given you?

- What aspect(s) of your current life might you be sidestepping? Are there areas of life—health, family, faith—you aren't confronting?

- Will accepting this partnership allow you to align the ultimate purpose you identified with your daily actions? Will it present you with new opportunities to serve God and His creation?

The process of answering these questions revealed to him that there are always tradeoffs to be made. On the one hand, his skill sets were a perfect fit with the partnership opportunity. He felt good about the impact he could have on his clients and colleagues. On the other hand, he was concerned about how the travel demands of his current role occasionally had a negative impact on his family and health. He struggled honestly with several questions. Could he, by accepting this partnership, rewrite those chapters of his life that were unsatisfying? Would the move enhance or detract from fulfilling his responsibilities to family, health, and vocation? If the salary in this new position were reduced by half, would he still make the same decision? How would this new role impact his relationship with God? Was this truly where God was calling him for the next decade?

I shared with my friend my own experience in the world of politics. The time I spent in this intensely competitive, time-consuming work convinced me that the political arena was not to be my permanent calling. I realized that to do my best in the world of politics, I would have to cut corners in one or more areas of my life. In the end, after prayerful consideration, I determined that God did not intend for me to achieve "success" in one calling at the expense of others that were equally as important. My friend ultimately accepted the partnership offer, knowing that he would have to commit to certain rituals in order to live out his complete life story with authenticity.

It is not always a tempting offer, such as the one my friend had, that moves us to assess our current vocational role. Often, it is personal tragedy. For Steven Biedermann, a 45-year-old investment banker from Chicago, September 11 was the catalyst. His work before that day provided financial reward, but little meaning. Following September 11, Steven sold everything, joined the Peace Corps, and went to Kiribati, in the Central Pacific, where he served others and grew in his relationship with God. Upon his return to Chicago, Steve drew on his banking skills and secured a job managing the investment portfolio of the Chicago public schools system. Even on a fraction of his former salary in banking, he has found peace in the knowledge that he has found his true calling. He comments, "It's about serving others, not being served. That's where my happiness comes from."[7]

Steve's honest assessment of his career serves as an example for us, as we seek and live out our professional calling. Take time to answer the following questions:

- What is the professional role to which God is calling me? Where do my skill sets and passion intersect with the needs of the world? Is my current story aligned with my quest to live a professional life of significance?

- What aspects of my professional story am I sidestepping? What portions of my life are too painful to confront? Am I effectively using my skill sets to double the talents God has given me? In what areas can I improve?

- What actions do I need to take to align my professional life with my ultimate purpose in life? What rituals can I implement to ensure that connection? Am I demonstrating my faith at work or at school?

Now, recall the diagram on which we can plot our story along present and future curves:

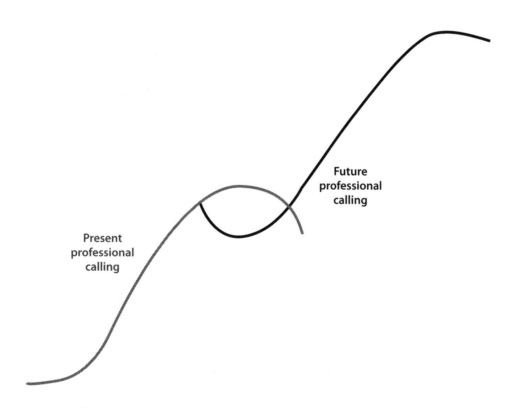

Utilizing this framework, we ask, "Who has God placed in my path to serve today?" and "What skill sets do I need to develop in order to live out the life God created uniquely for me in the future?" For example, into the path of a college student God places opportunities to serve classmates and teachers, as well as contributing to others through part-time work. He or she also studies, prepares for exams, and completes class projects, knowing that the quality of their efforts today impacts their life tomorrow.

Spend some moments thinking about how your skills and work in the present can impact your future work. Like yours, my future curve has a number of possibilities:

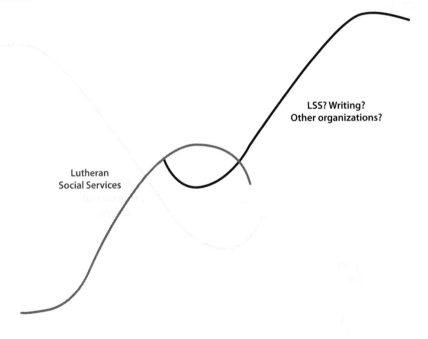

My favorite hobby is writing. Is it possible to make this a future career? I also enjoy consulting on behalf of other organizations. Is this where God is leading me? Lately, I feel God pulling me to become more involved with international relief work. I have opportunity to participate in the Lutheran Malaria Initiative. My participation in each has taught me new skills that enhance my work in my current profession.

My niece Katy's professional curve looks like this:

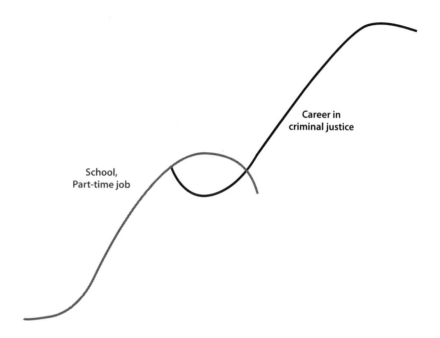

Katy, through her present-curve interactions with classmates, friends, family, teachers, and customers, wears the "mask" of God. She sees these interactions as preparation for what she believes may be her future calling as a police officer. She juggles school, work, and her role as a mother of an infant son to prepare her for the juggling she will have to do in the future. She knows that she must make good choices today so she can be well-positioned for her life of service tomorrow.

Take time now to sketch your present and future curves:

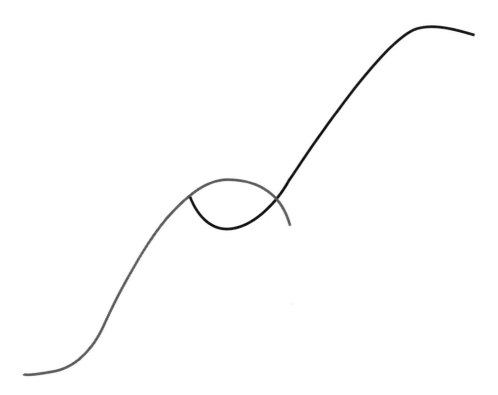

    I have determined the following as my priorities to help ensure that my current life's activities remain in line with my vision for life in the future:

- Live a life of simplicity

- Focus on keeping healthy—spiritually, physically, and emotionally

- Find time to write

- Use my talents to help an organization that serves clients in developing countries

- Proactively sharpen my current skill sets today so I will continue to add value to my work tomorrow

- Focus on serving well those I come into contact with today

- Remain open to new possibilities

Below, list those values you will focus on today that will position you to maximize your talents tomorrow:

1. _____

2. _____

3. _____

4. _____

5. _____

Again, we call on the findings of Mihaly Csikszentmihalyi, who describes the need to engage in purposeful challenges in order for us to feel fulfilled as human beings. Integrating his work into a Christian framework, we understand that our faith provides connecting order that transforms our professional vocation "into a single flow activity, with unified goals that provide constant purpose."[8] With that in mind, answer the following questions:

1. Who has God placed in my professional path to serve?

2. By what specific activities can I serve these individuals via my professional calling?

3. What rituals can I implement as daily reminders that every aspect of my work is significant in fulfilling my calling?

4. How can I remain alive to the fact that God can work good out of every experience, every situation.

Through the grace that flows from our Baptism, the Holy Spirit works in us and through us to shape our professional lives as *avodah*—an act of worship *and* service.

It is perhaps in our professional vocation that a life of simplicity is most challenging. Here we must make sure that our use of resources is aligned with our faith. Providing for our family is, of course, one important use of our resources. Our paycheck pays the monthly bills, and, we hope, provides extra money to enjoy our time off. Our financial resources make it possible for us to care for a family member who needs help. A promotion or pay increase means we can increase our giving to church and charitable causes. Out of necessity, a parent may work two jobs to give her children the chance to pursue their education and develop their talents—something she never had opportunity to do. Her call to this role is unselfish, and her income is a blessed source by which she folds her work into the life of significance she sees for her children.

For some, however, attachment to material goods is a stumbling block along the path to a life of significance. They allow their resources to control them as they mistake their needs with their wants. Or they feel trapped in their profession because they have become accustomed to a certain lifestyle. Such misplaced priorities can have disastrous consequences on our family, our health, and our faith. A life of simplicity, as I have defined it in this book, broadens our perspective and presents us with more opportunities to connect our passions to the needs of the world. When unmanageable ego is removed from the equation, when our lifestyle is de-coupled from the drive for more, our eyes are opened to a menu of possibilities that no longer focus on our needs alone.

It is vital for family members to talk about the value of living a life of simplicity, both individually and collectively. Laurie and I have included Sydney in our discussions about how remaining in our twenty-eight-year-old home that is nearly paid for has enabled us to afford a Christian high school for Sydney. We anticipate that living below our means will ensure that our financial support will remain constant as she pursues her goal to become a family and child therapist. It also enables Laurie to engage in meaningful volunteer activities. Similarly, driving our ten-year-old vehicle and shopping at inexpensive stores allows us to save money today so that money will not be the determining factor in deciding whether or not to accept a new position to which God may call me.

As we think about the line between living a life of simplicity and fulfilling our calling, it is helpful to consider the following questions:

- Are you in control of your lifestyle, or is it controlling you?

- Is your current lifestyle limiting the choices you are able to make in terms of your professional vocation?

- Is the prospect of monetary rewards, prestige, and security preventing you from putting God first?

- Have you and your family members talked about what it means to live a life of simplicity? Is each willing to commit to this goal? What would such a commitment look like for each member?

- Are you using your resources effectively to serve others? If not, what is getting in the way? What changes do you need to make to use your financial resources—whether $10,000 or $10 million—to further your worship of God and service to others?

As in other areas of our life, so too, with our professional calling, the importance of our health is vital. What rituals around caring for body, mind, and spirit might we develop that will allow us to perform in our vocation to our fullest potential? It might be something "easy" to incorporate, like a half-hour of daily exercise or an extra fifteen minutes in devotions. On occasion, the discernment process is more complex and demands a fearless look at our lives. Is our professional role having a negative impact on our personal integrity? Do we have a sense that God is calling us elsewhere, but are frozen by our fear of change? When we feel stress in one area of our life, the other areas suffer as well. It is an upset of *shalom*—the wholeness and peace—the balance God intended for us at creation, and which He re-creates by our Baptism. And it is in *shalom* that we receive Jesus' words, "Therefore I tell you, do not be anxious about your life . . . And do not seek what you are to eat and what you are to drink, nor be worried. For all the nations of the world seek after these things, and your Father knows that you need them. Instead, seek His kingdom, and these things will be added to you" (Luke 12:22, 29–31).

I have adapted Roy Oswald's Doing—Being chart to help us further assess the health of our professional calling.[9]

DOING Positives	BEING Positives
Serving a co-worker or customer.	Taking a well-deserved vacation.
Utilizing your passion to enhance a small piece of God's creation	
Successfully doubling the talent entrusted to you by your supervisor.	Balancing your work/family life.
Witnessing to co-workers via words and action.	Letting go of ego at work.
Enhancing your skill sets as you focus on your present and future curves.	Knowing that this is the vocation God created uniquely for you.
Strengthening your faith via your educational or professional calling.	Gaining wisdom.
DOING Negatives	**BEING Negatives**
Working long hours at the expense of your family or relationship with God.	God is no longer at the center of your life.
Neglecting your co-workers.	Lack of concern for your organization.
Compromising your integrity at work.	Excessive focus: "What's in it for me?"
Increase in physical or emotional ailments.	
Blaming others when things go wrong.	Dreading going to work.

If we are honest, even a quick review of the chart is revealing about the quadrant in which we operate. Even those of us who feel fulfilled in our current calling find ourselves in the negative quadrants on occasion. Sometimes, we have no choice. In response to Hurricane Katrina, a number of colleagues and I had to place other priorities on hold as we marshaled resources and administered the response efforts on behalf the nation's two largest Lutheran church bodies. The months of physical and emotional strain left us exhausted. We realized that in order to keep on doing the greatest good, we needed to employ those rituals that would help move us back into the positive territory. Only then would our ongoing help be truly helpful.

Below are a few of the rituals that, over time, have helped keep me grounded in the positive quadrants:

- Leave the office by 5:30 p.m. on days that I am not traveling.

- Never use work as an excuse for not attending church.

- Listen to my wife when she says I have said "yes" to too many commitments.

- Exercise at least four times a week.

- Schedule regular vacations with family.

- Eat at least two healthy meals each day.

- Devote at least 50 percent of my reading time to the Bible and other Christian books.

- Take time annually to discern whether my current role is still the most effective way for me to fulfill my ultimate purpose.

Now, list the rituals that you have or will implement to help you stay in positive territory:

1. _____

2. _____

3. _____

4. _____

5. _____

Even when we are engaged in what we believe to be our proper vocation, things don't always go as planned. The boss is unreasonable, the business fails, the commissioned sale doesn't materialize, our co-worker stabs us in the back, we are shunned for refusing to lie about the numbers, or someone else receives credit for our good work. The list goes on and on. Here, too, our relationship with God places us on solid ground. Gene Veith accurately reminds us, "Without faith, vocations are mere employments, mere things to do, empty of God and empty of meaning. Faith sees them as masks of God. Without faith, suffering is empty and purposeless, an example of the absurdity and meaningless of life. With faith, suffering in vocation becomes a cross, comprehended in the saving cross of Jesus Christ."[10]

Marc Kolden further explains:

> This notion of a cross in one's calling can assist us in making sense of failure, frustration, conflict and even tragedy in our work. We do not usually think of such negative experiences as giving anything "meaning," but Luther would advise us that this is a realistic way to look at life and work; therefore, these experiences, too, belong to the meaning of our work.[11]

God uses even our difficult situations to drive us back to the cross, back to prayer, and to discover new ways to serve. That which we experience as a burden can be the occasion for service in unforeseen ways.

Daily, we face dilemmas for which there are no easy solutions. A case worker in child protective services must decide whether to leave a child in the home of his biological parents whose care is questionable or bring him into the uncertain world of foster care. A small-business owner faces the no-win situation of having to fire an employee whose work is substandard, but who is also her family's sole breadwinner. A politician must search his conscience before voting on death penalty legislation. In my role at Lutheran Social Services, I have discovered that decisions that result in "ideal" outcomes are rare. On a moment's notice, we are asked to find someone willing to care for a dying child who has been abandoned by her parents. The answer to our prayer comes in the form of a faithful woman, with a somewhat tainted background, who steps forward now to care for this child in her final days. A friend once offered me this advice when I find myself facing such situations: Pray. Make my choice, then run to the cross as fast as I can! Good advice for us all who strive to serve God in a world littered with sin, suffering, abandonment, apathy, fear, and limited resources.

We occasionally need to be reminded that our professional life is not an end in itself. Sometimes we become addicted to our professional success, and only the ever-larger bonuses or business conquests will continue to satisfy. Or we may lose our identity in our professional roles. Neither our success nor our accomplishments will bring us closer to God. Work, as important as it is, does not define who we are or gives our life its ultimate worth. I play the part of a CEO, board chair, writer, speaker, and active participant in the political process. Others play the role of a pastor, professor, accountant, social worker, janitor, politician, waiter, or small-business owner. Each of us "wears" our identity. When we assign such labels to our tasks, we pigeonhole ourselves and make it difficult to engage in authentic human interaction.[12] As Eckhart Tolle reminds us, "The more identified people are with their respective roles, the more inauthentic the relationships become."[13]

To avoid this trap, we must constantly inquire whether we are performing our professional calling as a result of our ego. Are we at ease doing our work well without the need for accolades or attention? Are we truly satisfied in our vocation for no other reason than that it gives us purpose? When we perform even ordinary tasks to the best of our ability, we are powerful, for then we are wearing the mask of God, and our daily tasks become intertwined acts of service and worship. Tolle captures in secular terms this truth of our faith: "In essence you are neither inferior nor superior to anyone. True self-esteem and true humility arise out of that realization."[14] Or, as spoken by Jesus, "So the last will be first, and the first last" (Matthew 20:16). In another of life's paradoxes, the less our ego is a factor in our vocation, the more likely it is that we will have an impact far beyond our particular role or function.

Jack Fortin reminds us that, like the blind man in Mark 8, we all are, at times, in need of a "second touch by Jesus to really see."[15] Our faith enables us to see the endless possibilities to serve our neighbor through our professional vocation as we bring to the workplace a measure of trust, honesty, and integrity; implement policies of fairness and openness; and practice good stewardship. By looking outward, our need for attention diminishes. We gain new appreciation for our work as an offering of worship and service. Luther creatively describes this interconnectedness:

> If you are a manual laborer, you find that the Bible has been put in your workshop, into your hand, into your heart. It teaches and preaches how you should treat your neighbor. Just look at your tools—at your needle or thimble, your beer barrel, your goods, your scales or yardsticks or measure—and you will read this statement inscribed on them. Everywhere you look, it stares at you. Nothing that you handle every day is so tiny that it does not continually tell you this, if you will only listen. Indeed, there is no shortage of preaching. You have as many preachers as you have transactions, goods, tools, and other equipment in your house and home. All this continually crying out to you: "Friend, use me in your relations with your neighbor just as you would want your neighbor to use his property in his relations with you."[16]

Our professional vocation is our *avodah*, our work and worship, as collectively we care for God's creation. This is what it means to live a life of significance through the high calling of our daily work.

16

SERVING OUR COMMUNITY

A Christian lives not in himself, but in Christ and his neighbor. Otherwise he is not a Christian.
—Martin Luther[1]

A lawyer once asked Jesus, "Teacher, what shall I do to inherit eternal life?" Jesus answered by asking the lawyer, "What is written in the Law?" The lawyer replied, "You shall love the Lord your God with all your heart and with all your soul and with all your strength and with all your mind, and your neighbor as yourself." The lawyer, not knowing when to quit, presses on, "And who is my neighbor?" Jesus proceeded to tell the parable of the Good Samaritan (Luke 10:25–37). He could have chosen to answer the question abstractly, with no characters, no locations—no action! Instead, Jesus placed His story on a perilous, 13-mile stretch of road between Jerusalem and Jericho, probably akin to any crime-ridden area of a modern large city. He talked about a certain man who fell among thieves—today we might call them gang-bangers. Two men pass by, a priest and a Levite, and skip to the other side of the road. Then comes the Samaritan, and he alone aids the injured man. Jesus called this Samaritan "good." Martin Luther King Jr., commenting on the parable in his book, *The Measure of a Man*, relates that because the Jericho road was so dangerous, the priest and the Levite might easily have suffered the same beating as the man whom they ignored. King imagines that the two, on seeing the man in distress, may have asked themselves, "If I stop to help this man, what will happen to me?" But the Samaritan, by the very nature of his concern, reversed the question, "If I do not stop to help this man, what will happen to him?"[2] King reminds us that the Good Samaritan "was great because he had the mental equipment for dangerous altruism. He was great because he could surround the length of his life with the breadth of life. He was great because not only had he ascended to certain heights of economic security, but because he could condescend to the depths of human need."[3] Like the Samaritan, you and I fulfill our calling to serve our community when we develop the capacity to look beyond our own needs and care for our neighbors as we would care for ourselves.

Christ calls us to be His slaves. As such, we are not "free" to pass by on the other side. Rather, we are called to diminish our selves in order to see and to serve those in our paths—especially the injured and hurting. God's face shines through our service to others, and in our service, we are serving God. Jesus said, "For I was hungry and you gave Me food, I was thirsty and you gave Me drink, I was a stranger and you welcomed Me, I was naked and you clothed Me, I was sick and you visited Me, I was in prison and you came to Me. . . . Truly, I say to you, as you did it to one of the least of these My brothers, you did it to Me" (Matthew 25:35–36, 40).

Our salvation is by grace alone. However, the gift of salvation naturally bears good fruit, especially that of loving others by our words and actions. Our neighbors are in continual need of God's mercy, as are you and I. When we, as the hands and feet of Christ on earth, express the mercy of God, we are expressing our faith in action. Thus, the two words, *grace* and *mercy*, are used together in Scripture. Martin Luther explains:

> Faith is a living, daring confidence in God's grace, so sure and certain that the believer would stake his life on it a thousand times. This knowledge of and confidence in God's grace makes men glad and bold and happy in dealing with God and with all creatures. And this is the work which the Holy Spirit performs in faith. Because of it, and without compulsion, a person is ready and glad to do good to everyone, to serve everyone, to suffer everything, out of love and praise to God who has shown him this grace. Thus it is impossible to separate works from faith, quite as impossible to separate heat and light from fire.[4]

In a scene from Fyodor Dostoevsky's classic story, *The Brothers Karamazov*, Father Zossima is speaking with an insecure, wealthy woman, who is worried about whether or not there is eternal life. The priest admits that he cannot prove to her its existence. He goes on to explain that one can be convinced "by the experience of *active love*":

> Strive to love your neighbors actively and indefatigably. And the nearer you come to achieving this love, the more convinced you will become of the existence of God and the immortality of your soul. If you reach the point of complete selflessness in your love of your neighbors, you will most certainly regain your faith and no doubt can possibly enter your soul.[5]

Our life of faith begins in Baptism and is fed along the way by God's Word and by Christ's body and blood in the Lord's Supper. From this, says Rev. Matthew Harrison, "mercy spills out from the Sacraments onto our neighbors."[6]

God forgives, grants life, and empowers us for a life of meaning, which includes care for the sick, the abused, the poor, the hurting, and the disenfranchised.

Jesus taught that, while we are not "of" the world, we cannot escape being "in" the world. He said, "You are the salt of the earth, but if salt has lost its taste, how shall its saltiness be restored? It is no longer good for anything except to be thrown out and trampled under people's feet" (Matthew 5:13). To further explicate His point, He switched metaphors. "A city set on a hill cannot be hidden. Nor do people light a lamp and put it under a basket, but on a stand, and it gives light to all in the house. In the same way, let your light shine before others, so that they may see your good works and give glory to your Father who is in heaven" (Matthew 5:14–16). There is no question that we are called to serve by our good deeds. As the rays of a lamp spread away from the source, so our mercy shines away from us toward others. The Holy Spirit gives us outer focus and inner peace.

God forgives, grants life, and empowers us for a life of meaning.

Many of us embrace the idea of serving our community only half-heartedly, motivated by guilt rather than by deep compassion. We may choose to partake of all that the world has to offer, and ignore the reality that Christian discipleship does indeed come with a cost. Jesus thus instructed His disciples, "If the world hates you, know that it has hated Me before it hated you. If you were of the world, the world would love you as its own; but because you are not of the world, but I chose you out of the world, therefore the world hates you" (John 15:18–19). When we take seriously our call to be *in* the world and not *of* the world, our perspective on stewardship changes. Our understanding of what it means to serve community is transformed. Jesus gave us both a promise and a command: we are chosen by God to "go and bear fruit and that your fruit should abide, so that whatever you ask the Father in My name, He may give it to you. These things I command you, so that you will love one another" (John 15:16–17).

Society would have us believe that we "own" our wealth, that we are entitled to spend our assets as we see fit, that it is only out of the goodness of our heart that we even think of sharing with those less fortunate. But the Bible offers a different ethical dynamic and expectation. The Old Testament is filled with episodes of God showering bounty on His people. But God makes it clear that these blessings are intended for the whole community, not for just an individual. It was unimaginable that a single person would hoard his goods and enjoy them in isolation from other members of the community.[7] The prophets Malachi and Isaiah both declared that if God's people would open their hearts and obediently share their wealth with those who are in need, God would reward them with an abundance of material blessings.[8] Unfortunately, these words sometimes become twisted to fit a *quid pro quo* oriented faith: lead a godly life, and you will be materially blessed. The Bible is clear in its message that our material blessings are meant to be shared. We are blessed so that we can be a blessing to others.

Each of us is endowed with a multitude of gifts. Along with them come these rather ominous words from Jesus, "Everyone to whom much was given, of him much will be required, and from him to whom they entrusted much, they will demand the more" (Luke 12:48). Richard Foster offers this explanation of the relationship between our gifts and our obedience in using them:

> The deeper reality in obedience is the kind of spirit it works into us. It is a spirit that crucifies greed and covetousness. It is a spirit of compassion and outreach. It is a spirit of sensitivity and trust. Once this inner disposition has taken over our personality, material blessings cannot hurt us, for they will be used for right purposes. We will recognize material goods to be not for us alone, but for the good of all.[9]

The prophet Micah set forth the mission statement for our life toward community. "He has told you, O man, what is good; and what does the Lord require of you but to do justice, and to love kindness, and to walk humbly with your God" (6:8). Proverbs adds, "Whoever pursues righteousness and kindness will find life, righteousness, and honor" (21:21). The clear message rings throughout the New Testament, where Jesus exhorts us to be His "witnesses in

Jerusalem and in all Judea and Samaria, and to the end of the earth" (Acts 1:8). What a staggering command! Jesus also makes it clear that, without the Holy Spirit, we are not able to carry out the command (Acts 5:32; 22:15). With God at the center of our lives, we are well-positioned to be witnesses—beginning with where we live, yet trusting that our witness will reverberate beyond.

We can feel Jesus' frustration in His lament over the neglect of justice and mercy by people of faith:

> Woe to you, scribes and Pharisees, hypocrites! For you tithe mint and dill and cumin, and have neglected the weightier matters of the law: justice and mercy and faithfulness. These you ought to have done, without neglecting the others. You blind guides, straining out a gnat and swallowing a camel! (Matthew 23:23–24)

One wonders how Jesus would speak to us today. Would He say to us what He said to Peter: "Are you also still without understanding?" (Matthew 15:16). The Bible is unequivocal in its command to serve our community. We are called—right here, right now—to confront racism, sexism, environmental degradation, corrupt political systems, unfair judicial processes, hunger, poverty, inadequate education, disease, and insufficient access to health care; all this out of love.

There is so much suffering in the world that we sometimes become immune to it. We walk by the homeless man on the sidewalk, look past the stare of a hungry child, or close the newspaper at yet another story of a terrorist attack halfway across the globe. We must relearn—or perhaps learn for the first time—the compassion Jesus felt for our broken and hurting world. *Splanchnon* is the Greek word for such compassion. Rev. Matthew Harrison describes how, in pre-Christian usage, *splanchnon* "denoted the 'inward parts' of a sacrifice, such as the 'liver, lungs, and spleen.' It also denoted the . . . womb or the loins. In more figurative usage, and for obvious reasons, the word meant 'the seat of impulsive passions.' "[10] Harrison goes on to explain that, for Jesus, compassion is literally "visceral." Every instance where *splanchnon* is used in the New Testament to describe Jesus' compassion is followed by an action of mercy. We might say that Jesus had *gut-wrenching* compassion for the hungry when he fed the 5,000 (Matthew 14:13–21); healed the two blind men (Matthew 20:29–34); cleansed the leper (Mark 1:40–45); healed the boy with an unclean spirit (Mark 9:14–29); and raised the widow's son (Luke 7:11–17).[11] To fulfill our calling to our community, we must experience such gut-wrenching compassion, then follow with intentional acts of mercy.

There is so much suffering
in the world that we sometimes
become immune to it.

How often do we keep our distance from a neighbor in need, avoiding eye contact for fear that that we will be expected to help? Our self-indulgence keeps us from seeing the hurting person as a child of God, made in God's image. He or she is you and me! He or she deserves our full attention and compassion—our *splanchnon*. What would our life look like if we took seriously Christ's call to His ambassadors to everyone we meet? Into what new type of human relationships would our actions of love lift us? What if we behaved like Abraham and Sarah, gladly serving complete strangers, welcoming them into our home as if it were God whom we welcomed (Genesis 18:1–33)? The opposite of love is not hate—it is selfishness. Our focus on self becomes the barrier to living a life of significance. When Jesus called the disciples from their work on the seashore, it was not with qualifications. He did not say, "You will be fishers only of the people on your street." Jesus' call was to cast their nets for *all* people, to seek to help everyone, neighbor by neighbor. It is a tall order, for if we take His words seriously, then we understand that everyone is our neighbor—the co-worker who irks us; the most unpopular student in our class; the immigrant family next door; the brother we don't get along with; the confused grandmother in the nursing home; the child dying of malaria; the mother in Africa who can't find suitable drinking water for her family.

The Eight Strategies

By now, we have seen how the Eight Strategies can be useful tools in our quest to bring our actions and our "selves" into alignment with our ultimate purpose in life. When confronted with opportunities to show acts of mercy, the strategies, drawing upon the teaching of the Scriptures, lead us to ask, "If I do not stop and help the hurting in my community, what will happen to them?" Our beginning point is, as always, our relationship with God. God welcomed us in Baptism and established with us a covenant of compassion. We, then, can welcome others, thereby creating a bridge on which we meet them in their suffering. We begin to comprehend that our relationship with God and our compassion toward others are inseparable, that the Holy Spirit fuses our faith and our service into a unique circle of mercy. We pause for a moment to ask:

- What does my current life of service to others say about the nature of my relationship with God?

- Who are my neighbors?

- Can others know, by my actions, that I am a Christian?

- In what ways can I help ensure that the light of my faith shines brightly toward others?

- What acts of service can I perform this week through which the Holy Spirit may enhance my faith?

A faith that is secure in Christ sees opportunities for service everywhere. The eyes of our heart are opened to numerous possibilities—from the need to start a recycling program to caring for an injured pet to driving an elderly neighbor to the doctor. We see how the dots in our constellation are really clusters of opportunity for service—how, through our influence in one sphere of our life we can show compassion to those in other spheres. The examples to do so are endless. We can connect an under-employed church member in need of a construction job with a business associate who is looking to remodel his home; provide legal advice for free to those who can't afford to pay; use our electrical skills to rewire an old home in danger of electrical disaster; connect a wealthy colleague with a worthy charity; ask a friend to volunteer with us at the local food bank. Fifteen years ago, my friend Bob Miles introduced me to a young pastor by the name of John Nunes. "It would be good if the two of you could work together someday," Bob said, by way of introduction. Little did any of us know the relationship would result in John and me working closely together on numerous community projects, including the Lutheran Malaria Initiative. By connecting the dots within his spheres of influence, Bob was able to make an impact that far exceeded what he might have accomplished on his own.

A faith that is secure in Christ sees opportunities for service everywhere.

Take time now to think about how, through the galaxy of your various relationships, you can serve your community. List several possibilities:

1. _____

2. _____

3. _____

4. _____

5. _____

Looking at your list above, you will likely see gaps between those opportunities and how you currently operate in your social, business, and family spheres. The difference between who we say we want to be and who we are is greater than we would like. We can move toward closing this gap by naming certain rituals and applying them in our plan to serve. Ask yourself, "What would it look like if I dared to live seriously Christ's call to serve my community?" For example, your goals might include the following:

- I will volunteer for a specific nonprofit organization, such as _____.

- I will increase my charitable giving by 1 percent each year for the next five years.

- I will identify one person (name him or her) in whose life I can make a real difference, and serve him or her over the next twelve months.

- I will daily seek out persons who are in need of a prayer, a word of encouragement, or some other action of compassion.

- I will participate in a mission trip this year.

- I will live a lifestyle that enables me to give more of my time and resources on behalf of others.

Honestly assess whether your current lifestyle allows for these goals. Where are the gaps? What rituals do we need to implement to make the necessary changes? Take time now to visualize your "ideal" life of service to community. What is preventing you from that life? Take a moment to list those things:

1. _____

2. _____

3. _____

4. _____

5. _____

To tell the "story" of our community service honestly, we must confront those areas of our life that are keeping us from our goals. What idols are we serving—an expensive new home that is eating up our discretionary dollars? Undue preoccupation with a hobby that carves away time we could spend with others? A gentleman I know recently "re-read" his story, and didn't like what he saw as the underlying narrative—that watching football on television was running his life, stealing time and energy from that which is truly important. He explained that he used football as an excuse not to get involved. On Saturday, he had to watch the college games. He spent Sunday, Monday, and Thursday nights glued to the professional games on the screen. He spent countless hours playing fantasy football. He was forced to admit that this addiction was interfering with his ability to live a life of significance. As a result of this honest assessment, he gave up watching football all together. Now, he laughs when he tells me he realizes that "the same team wins whether or not I watch the game!"

The bottom-line question for those who have been blessed with wealth, perhaps by family inheritance, the result of the sweat and tears of running a small business, or the good fortune of profitable stock options is "How can we best use our wealth as an act of worship to God and actions of service to others?" The Scriptures are replete with references to the relationship between our money and how we choose to use our money in a world where poverty is the norm. The challenge is startling. How can we work toward equity, when more than one billion of the earth's inhabitants subsist on less than a dollar a day, while the average annual per capita in the U.S. is $30,000?[12] Paul instructs his young protégé, Timothy, "As for the rich in this present age, charge them not to be haughty, nor to set their hopes on the uncertainty of riches, but on God, who richly provides us with everything to enjoy. They are to do good, to be rich in good works, to be generous and ready to share, thus storing up treasure for themselves as a good foundation for the future, so that they may take hold of that which is truly life" (1 Timothy 6:17–19). Regardless of our particular standing, each of us needs reminding that "It is more blessed to give than to receive" (Acts 20:35); that our giving is to be systematic, according to a plan (2 Corinthians 16:2); that each should give according to his or her means (2 Corinthians 8:3; 11–13); that our giving is a privilege (2 Corinthians 8:4); it is a witness to the Gospel (2 Corinthians 8:8, 24); it is to be undertaken cheerfully (2 Corinthians 9:7); that it brings glory to God (2 Corinthians 9:11–13); and that giving is about more than money—it begins with committing our "selves" to the Lord (2 Corinthians 8:5).[13]

Martin Luther said that every person is in need of conversion of the heart, the mind, and the purse. It is often said that we should give from the heart. Mark Allen Powell urges us to develop a strategy that enables us to give *where we want our heart to be*. "Give to things you *should* care about, and your generosity will awaken the caring in your heart that you hope to find there."[14] In so doing, we can shift our priorities, looking outward, looking to our neighbors in need, and asking, "If I do not help, what will happen to them?" Take an honest look at your life as it is currently. Is your giving truly based on the question, "Where do I want my heart to be?" This attitude of the heart loosens self-imposed restrictions on our dollars, and allows us to see our way clear to make that first stretch gift. If your usual gift to a worthy cause is $1,000, make it $5,000. As our good friends Mildred and Lawrence Lieder regularly remind Laurie and me, "This isn't our money that we are donating to Lutheran Social Services, this is God's money. Don't thank us, thank God!"

By basing our giving on strategic planning, it makes it possible for our giving to serve our community—locally, regionally, and internationally. Our family frames our conversations about stewardship according to such a plan. We determine to whom, and on what level, our giving habits are directed:

Locally—in Austin, Texas, to individuals who are daily placed in our path, to Concordia Academy, Redeemer Lutheran Church and School, Meals on Wheels, Concordia University Texas, the Austin Humane Society, and the Austin Area Food Bank

Regionally—to Lutheran Social Services of the South, Valparaiso University, and mission trips sponsored by our congregation

Internationally—to sponsor a missionary, support Lutheran World Relief, and donate to Water to Thrive

Each year we pray about how we can do more than the year before, as we strive to multiply the talents God has entrusted to us. We remain open to new possibilities for service, and create habits of attention and awareness to opportunities for giving in a myriad of "routine" ways.

Either individually, or as a family, list the names of organizations in each of the following levels that you will support financially, and/or with your acts of service:

Local: _____

_____

Regional: _____

_____

International: _____

_____

In serving our neighbors, we are fulfilling our purpose as God's people. When we focus on others, we minimize the influence of our self-serving ego. An important part of responsible giving is to set clear goals. Dick Moeller is a great example. After hearing a presentation on the need for water wells in Ethiopia, Dick felt called to expand the initiative to other congregations. In the process, he established the nonprofit organization Water To Thrive as the structure for accomplishing his goal. Our goal, whether big or small, a long-term or a one-time commitment, is where we want our heart to be—it is where we become immersed in opportunity to be the hands and feet of Christ.

Living a life of simplicity helps set boundaries around our decisions as we pursue our call to serve community. In living such a life, led by the power of the Holy Spirit, we can refrain from getting caught up in the distractions and temptations of the world, and can disassociate ourselves from the pride that comes with the amount of money we have in the bank, the size of our home, or the brand of our automobile. By a faithful and humble lifestyle, we become wrapped up in the countless ways we can help others. We may even surprise ourselves! In our household, we have chosen to sacrifice going out to dinner for one month and to use the savings to purchase necessary items for a missionary. On her birthday, our daughter asks that friends bring to her party gifts to donate to a children's emergency shelter. We help mobilize fellow church members to raise money to build a well in Kenya, and go on a mission trip. In all of these—and the thousands of other examples you could list—we strive to treat each person—and each other—as a unique creation of God.

In serving our neighbors, we are fulfilling our purpose as God's people.

It is well documented that there is a direct, positive correlation between serving our community and our personal health.[15] Stephen G. Post, director of the Center for Medical Humanities, Compassionate Care and Bioethics, at Stony Brook University on Long Island, observes, "There's no question that [service] gives life a greater meaning when we make this kind of shift in the direction of others and get away from our own self-preoccupation and problems . . . But it also seems to be the case that there is an underlying biology involved in all this."[16] Conversely, scientific research has also shown that being self-centered may actually damage your health.[17] Some health practitioners are even beginning to "prescribe" caring for others as part of their treatment plan. When she was thirty-one years old, Cami Walker was diagnosed with multiple sclerosis. On the advice of a member of her health-care team, Cami gave one gift each day for a month. The gifts were small and simple—a phone call for support, a piece of chocolate cake to a friend. Cami details what she discovered in *29 Gifts: How a Month of Giving Can Change Your Life*. Her habit of giving did not cure her disease. But, she says, over that time period, she became less dependent, more mobile, and she found that her pain was more manageable—with less pain medication. The flare-ups stopped and scans show that her disease is no longer progressing.[18] My point in relating this is not to suggest that we should serve others so that we can improve our own health. However, Cami's story is an example of the mystery and wonder of God's creation, and of the possibilities for service to others that arise from our own difficult experiences.

Our ability to walk in humility, to be aware of our neighbors' needs, and to respond with compassion, means we must orient our values and goals with those of Jesus. God does not command us to obtain wealth or to achieve greatness. Instead, He expects us—and He makes us able—to be the good Samaritan, to feed the hungry, to invite in the stranger, to look after the sick, to clothe those in need, to visit the imprisoned. In the person of Jesus, God meets us along our path of sin and suffering, and continually restores us by His compassion. It is not a burden; it is His joy to do so. In the same way, our service to others, when done in the name of Christ, is not burdensome; it is a privilege. In a sense, serving others well may be the most "selfish" thing we do. For it is when we serve our community that we are following Christ and living a life of significance.

As we close this section I offer you a prayer that is commonly referred to as the Franciscan Blessing:

May God bless you with a restless discomfort about easy answers, half-truths, and superficial relationships, so that you may seek truth boldly and love deep within your heart.

May God bless you with holy anger at injustice, oppression, and exploitation of people, so that you may tirelessly work for justice, freedom, and peace among all people.

May God bless you with the gift of tears to shed with those who suffer from pain, rejection, starvation, or the loss of all that they cherish, so that you may reach out your hand to comfort them and transform their pain into joy.

May God bless you with enough foolishness to believe that you really CAN make a difference in this world, so that you are able, with God's grace, to do what others claim cannot be done.

And the blessing of God the Supreme Majesty and our Creator, Jesus Christ the Incarnate Word who is our brother and Saviour, and the Holy Spirit, our Advocate and Guide, be with you and remain with you, this day and forevermore.

Amen.

17

SERVING OUR CHURCH

For where two or three are gathered in My name,
there am I among them.
—**Matthew 18:20**

n our attempt to squeeze 28 hours of responsibilities into a 24-hour day, it is often the church that suffers. We all—myself included—know that truth, and have let slide the biblical injunction of "not neglecting to meet together, as is the habit of some, but encouraging one another, and all the more as you see the Day drawing near" (Hebrews 10:25). A lackadaisical attitude about our level of involvement in the church can result in a hard heart and a dull spirit. It is no wonder that is the case, since we are cutting ourselves off from the life source of our faith—exposure to God's Word and to the Sacrament of the Altar.

The further removed we are from this source, it seems, the more overwhelming temptation appears and the more easily strife creeps into our life. All this is collateral damage of not participating actively as part of the community of believers. As Donald Heiges aptly observes, "unless Christians take their calling seriously within the church there is not much hope of their taking it seriously in the world."[1] These are vital words to contemplate as we examine how participating in our congregation impacts our ability to follow God's call.

The congregation to which we belong—which is the local expression of Christ's Church on earth—is where we can both serve and be served. Here we avail ourselves of the means through which the Holy Spirit operates to forgive sin and strengthen our faith. Here we listen, worship, study, pray, and sing. In the pew (or the chair) we look to our pastor for faithful explanation of the Scriptures from the pulpit, and we look around us to our fellow members of the Body of Christ. It is primarily in the context of the worshiping community that we find grace to be forgiven and then forgive others, to receive help and then be a help to our neighbor, to be blessed and become a blessing to those who need it. To use the language set forth in this book, it is in staying connected to our local church that we live out our life in the flow of our Baptism. From this, the Holy Spirit makes us able to connect our dots in proper priority, tell our story honestly and fearlessly, construct our present and future curves, properly focus on the doing/being aspects of our lives, and live a life of simplicity and significance centered in the cross of Christ.

God commands our life of worship. In response to Satan's temptation of Jesus to dethrone God, our Lord says, "It is written, 'You shall worship the Lord your God, and Him only shall you serve' " (Luke 4:8). Jesus leaves no doubt that He and the Father are one: "This is the work of God, that you believe in Him whom He has sent" (John 6:29), and that by this work of God, we "may have life in His name" (John 20:31). True faith "comes from hearing, and hearing through the word of Christ" (Romans 10:17). God calls ministers to preach the Gospel message of salvation through Christ and to administer the Sacraments. The Holy Spirit works faith in those who hear the Gospel. Worship is not what we do for God. Rather, it is what God does for us. Jesus explains, "The Sabbath was made for man, not man for the Sabbath" (Mark 2:27). Worship promotes spiritual, mental, and physical restoration that serves to strengthen us and make us fit to wear the mask of God in service to others.

In Acts, we have this prosaic picture of the fellowship of believers: "And they devoted themselves to the apostles' teaching and the fellowship, to the breaking of bread and the prayers" (2:42). Through His Church, God provides all that is necessary for joyful living on earth and for an eternal life of praise in heaven. Our congregation supports us in our walk of faith. In addition to—and in support of—its functions of preaching the Gospel and providing the Sacraments, our congregation plays four roles to assist us in living a life of significance. First, it teaches us about our Christian faith. Through a variety of worship styles, class structures, small-group studies, confirmation classes, and preschool programs, the church provides opportunity to learn from the Word of God. Through this participation we are enlightened, energized, and empowered to serve in the different arenas of our life. Second, our congregation is a shelter, an enclave from the temptations and values of the postmodern world. It is an environment where you and I can establish deep friendships with other Christians. Third, our congregation is a safe haven in time of need. Certainly, there are counselors and therapists who can help us when we struggle with divorce, death, depression, or other loss. But in our congregation we discover those who can offer to us the compassion that is modeled after Christ. Finally, our congregation is the natural venue to organize our collective provision of acts of mercy. There exists a volunteer structure, the sole purpose of which is to serve those "within our walls," as well as those in our community—or across the ocean—who are in need.

The Church is ever in danger of being seen merely as a gathering of people dedicated to a good cause. Perhaps even more harmful is the mindset in today's society, described by sociologist Robert Bellah, which perceives the Church as just another consumer good. He describes how " 'Consumer Christians' shop for the church that is most convenient for their needs and switch, as casually as they change brands of dishwater detergent, if they think they can get a better package elsewhere."[2] We choose one church over another not because we genuinely believe our gifts could be better used elsewhere but because the pastor is more inspiring, the worship style more entertaining, the music more contemporary, or the location more convenient. To integrate our church life into our quest to live a life of significance requires that we see our congregation as the place where God is fully present and worthy of our worship. It is where we gather at the foot of the cross and from there are sent forth. We are privileged to assist our deaconess in calling on shut-ins, serving on the board of trustees, or singing in the choir. Of course, there may be times when we need what the church has to offer by way of counseling, financial support, or meeting space for a 12-step group. In both our giving to the church and our receiving, we discover within the Body of Christ how we can live "significant" lives as God's baptized.

Through His Church, God provides all that is necessary for joyful living on earth and for an eternal life of praise in heaven.

I personally continue to find immense purpose by my association with my church denomination. In the spirit of full disclosure, I serve on my denomination's national board of directors. I value the benefits of adhering to a common set of beliefs, engaging in a common mission, and using its pooled resources to create and support seminaries, schools, hospitals, publishing houses, fraternal organizations, social service agencies, and a global mission initiative. I value the privilege of being part of a church body that responds swiftly and effectively to ease suffering in natural disasters, pursues church planting, and takes seriously its responsibility to hold its leaders accountable for their actions. I also realize that the denomination to which I belong is a human organization, and therefore, less than perfect. It is often fraught with theological tension, cumbersome bureaucratic structures, and a slowness to adapt to the world's changing needs—especially those of the younger generation.

As we fulfill our vocation to serve our congregation, it is our challenge to combine the best of the old and the new as we strive to remain faithful to the Scriptures, yet flexible enough to be relevant in this rapidly changing world. *Christianity Today* reports that young people are leading "four small, but vital, movements energizing the Western church." The first is the "emerging" stream—those committed to reaching out to a population that is unlikely ever to attend a traditional church. The second is a "missional" stream—its purpose being to remind the Church of its identity as a *sent* Church. The third movement is defined as a "mosaic," which is characterized as younger people planting multicultural churches. The fourth movement is identified as "monastics"— young people dedicated to working with, and living in community with, the poor.[3] In my interactions with people in these movements, I have learned that we share one overarching priority: to be faithful, authentic people of integrity, desiring to integrate discipleship and stewardship in every aspect of our lives. Whether we serve a congregation, work on behalf of a denomination, or meet for prayer over coffee, we are united in our efforts to be *countercultural*, to live Christ-filled lives of significance through our worship and our service.

The Greek word for Church in the New Testament is *ekklesia*. Douglas Schuurman explains that "*ek* (from, out of) and *klesia*, (*klesis*, calling) together define the church as the assembly of 'called out ones.' As members of our church we are 'people called out of the world by God to serve God in the world.' "[4] Regrettably, many congregations pay scant attention to the needs of the outside world. The Atlanta-based Carter Center's Interfaith Health Program found that only 10 percent of congregations are actively focused on improving their community. Its director, Gary Gunderson, explains, "Helping people isn't done a hundred at a time; it is done one by one by one. The congregations that open themselves to the real needs of people stop talking at them and start talking *with* them—coming along beside them, becoming involved in their lives."[5]

A congregation provides the natural organizational construct to live out what Jesus names as the two greatest commandments: "You shall love the Lord your God with all your heart and with all your soul and with all your mind and with all your strength" and, "You shall love your neighbor as yourself" (Mark 12:30–31). We cannot love God and, at the same time, not love and serve our neighbor. If we are true to our faith and calling, we take seriously the model of mutual Christian care portrayed in Acts, where "there was not a needy person among them" (Acts 4:34). The structure of our congregation allows us to serve as "dots of influence," connecting members to one another and to the needs of the community. Gunderson reminds us that congregations have a unique capacity to connect people across economic lines and beyond the confines of our extended family connections. They have the ability to enhance health and wholeness—both among its members as well as outside its walls within the community.[6]

How we participate in our church calling has the potential to impact every aspect of our life. It nourishes our spirit for joyful service in all our vocations. We begin our week refreshed in our worship and energized for the days of service ahead. It strengthens us to be countercultural. By regular participation in the life of the Church, we are empowered to heed the words of St. Paul in his letter to the Romans:

> I appeal to you therefore, brothers, by the mercies of God, to present your bodies as a living sacrifice, holy and acceptable to God, which is your spiritual worship. Do not be conformed to this world, but be transformed by the renewal of your mind, that by testing you may discern what is the will of God, what is good and acceptable and perfect. (Romans 12:1–2)

The power of the Word and Sacraments provide us with the courage to live in our present-day Babylon, witnessing by deed and word to strangers, and thus fulfill the Great Commission: "Go therefore and make disciples of all nations, baptizing them in the name of the Father and of the Son and of the Holy Spirit" (Matthew 28:19).

The Strategies

A strategic approach to our calling to serve the Church helps us organize and hold ourselves accountable to our goals. A healthy connection to our congregation can impact both the positive "being" and the positive "doing" aspects of our life. We know from multiple research studies that those who regularly attend church are more likely to be healthier and live longer. I will close this section by sharing with you the following rituals to which I have committed myself in the year ahead. These are ways I have identified to help close the gap between how I am currently involved in my congregation and the level I want to be involved:

- To the extent my travel schedule allows, take advantage of all spiritual nourishment opportunities—Sunday School, worship, Communion, Advent and Lenten services, weekly Bible study.

- Develop closer friendships with members of my congregation.

- Get involved in one additional community project my congregation sponsors.

- Support the ministry of our new youth director.

- Connect dots of influence to solve an individual or community need.

In the space below, list the rituals you will commit to that will strengthen your call to serve your congregation.

1. _____

2. _____

3. _____

4. _____

5. _____

18

EMBRACING OUR SUFFERING TO DISCOVER OUR CALLING

And we know that for those who love God
all things work together for good, for those who
are called according to His purpose.

—Romans 8:28

Society in general derides the belief that suffering can be a positive force in our lives. We are told that we are entitled to have it all—often at no cost. "Just Do It!" as the slogan goes. We hear that we don't deserve the bad that happens to us. And, when our own lives going smoothly, we minimize the reality of the suffering of others, assigning it as something that befalls them—never to us. Put bluntly, we deceive ourselves into thinking that we are immune to suffering, forgetting that it is part of our lot in a world broken by sin. Into this great confusion, the Scriptures speak a word of clarity: God works through suffering to strengthen our faith, to give us wisdom, and to even help us discover new purpose in life. Paying attention to—and even embracing—our suffering is imperative if we are to live out our life's calling.

> God works through suffering to strengthen our faith, to give us wisdom, and to even help us discover new purpose in life.

The apostle Paul relates that he lived with a "thorn" in his flesh, which we can infer as some sort of severe, chronic affliction. He pleaded with God to take it away. God's response was "no." But it didn't end there. "My grace is sufficient for you, for My power is made perfect in weakness." "Therefore," Paul continues, "I will boast all the more gladly of my weaknesses, so that the power of Christ may rest upon me. . . . For when I am weak, then I am strong" (2 Corinthians 12:7–12). For Paul, as well as for each of us, illness, pain, and weakness can become blessings. The myriad of trials we endure bring us back to the cross, back to the Suffering One, by whose wounds we are healed. On the road of suffering discipleship, we discover our paths of significance.

It is easy to be thankful when good things come our way—the winning field goal, the promotion, the new home. Indeed, these can be blessings from God. It is not so easy—in fact, it is against all common sense—to believe that it is precisely in our trials that we experience God's presence most clearly. When we go through difficult times, we become more vulnerable and are forced to face the fact that we are not in control. It is then that we are more receptive to God's work and will. Our sufferings, failures, and losses are opportunities for the growth of our spirit. Reverend James McKibbin illuminates the point: "We are actually blessed when we have lost what is most dear to us. Because it is only then that we can be embraced by the one dearest to us."[1]

Martin Luther reminds us that there are two times in our life when we come closest to knowing God: when we suffer personally, and when we focus on the earthly suffering of Jesus. It is through the cross of Christ that we discover a God who has chosen to join our suffering, through the weakness, suffering, and death of His Son.[2] The Christian understanding of suffering is counter to the world's understanding—even though suffering may be burdensome, it can be a source of immense blessing. Difficulties can wear away our self-importance and open us to the working of God. Martin Luther said that suffering is nothing less than our living God working out the salvation in our lives.[3] It drives us back to the cross.

> The Christian understanding of suffering is counter to the world's understanding—even though suffering may be burdensome, it can be a source of immense blessing.

Over the years, many family members, friends, and acquaintances have either personally suffered tragedy or are close to others who have. The list seems overwhelming: destruction of a home by a hurricane, desertion by a spouse, a child killed in a car accident, a diagnosis of multiple sclerosis, loss of a job, suicide, addiction to drugs, a debilitating stroke, and the murder of a woman and her two sons by the husband and father. In response to these, there is no good answer for the question "Why?" Out of such tragedy comes opportunity to serve. Our Baptism makes us members of the caring body of Christ, and it is at such moments as these that we can offer our service. Without the hope that the Gospel gives us, our sufferings would surely be our undoing. But we can grasp the promises of God's presence and strength to help in our mutual task of Christian care.

Sometimes we bring our own suffering upon us. Lifestyle choices can bring about stress-related maladies, illness, and disease, such as strokes, heart disease, AIDS, cirrhosis of the liver, and many others. The number of deaths caused by drinking and driving increases every year. The break up of a marriage leaves children as victims. Regardless of the cause, God promises that nothing can separate us from His love in Christ. Luther reminds us that, through repentance, even the sufferings that we bring upon ourselves become truly "sanctified" and a blessing that brings us to Jesus.[4] In repentance, we approach God humbly, confident that He will not only forgive but also transform the troubles we have brought upon ourselves into new beginnings. We willingly bear the cross, secure in the knowledge that through it Christ will lead us ultimately to where there is no longer any pain or suffering.

> Without the hope that the Gospel gives us, our sufferings would surely be our undoing. God promises that nothing can separate us from His love in Christ.

There is a sense in which our suffering re-creates us—opens our hearts to new ways that God may be calling us. Douglas Schuurman explains, "Often it is in the dark nights of the soul, or in the brightness of an experience of God's presence, that we perceive God's callings."[5] Affliction may bring a kind of death in one area of our life. But it also is the possibility of a new beginning for us—a move to a different community, the chance to see a broken relationship through new eyes, the ability to identify more closely with another who has experienced a similar loss. The story of the patriarch Jacob is the story of each of us. Before crossing the river to be reunited with his twin, Esau, Jacob spent the night wrestling the angel of the Lord. At dawn's break, the angel "touched" Jacob's hip, giving him a limp as a painful reminder of his epic struggle. But the angel also gave him a great blessing by changing his name to Israel—the one through whom God would continue the line of descendants, leading ultimately to Jesus (Genesis 32:22–32). The psychological and physical scars we bear from our struggles may never completely heal, but through them, God gives unforeseen blessings. Out of the tragic death of Jesus on the cross comes our greatest blessing.

How we respond to life's challenges determines how we embrace our life of significance. Deluding ourselves with the thought that we shouldn't have to suffer only intensifies our pain, for then we are living in complete denial. We must consciously accept our suffering before we can transcend it.[6] In my position at Lutheran Social Services, I have been privileged to spend many hours with people whose lives have been devastated by flood, hurricane, or other natural disaster. I have seen how some individuals become bitter and resentful, and perhaps turn to alcohol and violence, as they seek ways to deal with their anger and grief. Some say such disasters are signs of God's wrath upon "heathen" populations. Others lash out at family and friends, and still others unleash their anger on well-meaning disaster responders, who are unable to fulfill unrealistic expectations for reconstruction.

Others choose a different path and humbly accept what befalls them, not as hopeless victims, but in the knowledge that the peace of God transcends even this crisis. They can embrace the indignity of their plight, rejoice at the kindness of the volunteers, and offer to help those who have come to help them. I have known some who perceive their personal tragedy as a gift, for without it, they would still be living by desperate attachment to their material possessions. In our suffering, as in all areas, we can find opportunity to reconnect the dots, establish new rituals, write a new chapter, and live a more simple life. It is a new start for a life of significance.

Sometimes, an event in our life is so powerful we can't ignore the message. Lutheran Social Services partners with a former Fortune 500 executive who was involved in a horrific car accident that could easily have killed her. While recuperating in the hospital, she came to recognize that the lucrative position she held at the time was no longer the work she felt called to do. Not long this realization she resigned, acted on her passion that combined her love of children and for horses, and established a ranch that provides horse therapy for disabled and at-risk children. For others, it may take a heart attack or a troubled teenage child before they open their eyes to the possibility of a new career or other major life change. It may take a life-shattering event—literally—to shock us out of the trench our ego has dug. On solid ground once again, we kneel at the cross, open to a new vision for our future.

The pain we experience in one area of our life sometimes contributes to a life of greater significance in another area. *Time* magazine correspondent Michael Weisskopf poignantly writes about how it took having his right hand blown off in Iraq to find his true calling. His injury triggered him to look inside—to realize that, in essence, he derived his self-worth from who he was and not from his career as a well-known journalist. It helped him rediscover how his vocations as spouse, father, brother, and son were as important as his professional vocation. His injury forced him to see how, in pursuing thrills and putting himself in danger, he didn't see the cost to his family.[7] Weisskopf's journey is a reminder of how setbacks give us the opportunity to view life differently.

How we respond to life's challenges determines how we embrace our life of significance.

When we suffer the loss of someone or something we love, we also lose a part of ourselves. It is a time of great vulnerability. We might rage against God, blame others, feel entitled, or live in resentment. Sometimes it takes going through these events to bring us to a place of humility, where we turn to God, ready to hear His call to a different kind of life. Suffering brings change. This does not come about because of our long-suffering or courage. Rather, as we fall on trembling knees and ask for His leading, God transforms us into persons with renewed faith and passion, ready to envision new possibilities.

The Strategies

Like the mother who after undergoing the pain of childbirth is awakened to a maternal instinct she never knew existed, we through our suffering may become more alive to aspects of ourselves that had been dormant. First and foremost, our periods of suffering are natural reminders that God is in control and desires to be at the center of our life. Living with chronic pain or mental illness are daily reminders that we live in a broken world. Yet, through our pain, we discover avenues by which God blesses us, and we can bless others.

In our suffering, we are invited to redefine our purpose in life. A traumatic event presents us with a "do-over"—a chance to step back, assess our story, and write future chapters in the book that is our life. We can close the gap between the person we are today and the person God intends us to be. We can see how a crisis jumbles up our constellation of dots so that some are removed, others added, and some rearranged. We can discern in this re-formed constellation how we can serve individuals who had not been in our lives before.

Sometimes God uses the aches and pains of old age, a fading memory, or a terminal illness to remind us that we are running out of time to close the gap between our present and future curves. As we near death, new priorities appear— to draft a will, plan our funeral, or make arrangements so that our children won't be burdened with our home and business obligations. We may need to attend to those from whom we need forgiveness, or whom we need to forgive. When we view our life along the two curves, we can see how the decisions we make today prepare us for the challenges of tomorrow.

What obstacles are facing you currently? Take time to think about a particular challenge you are experiencing. How has this "upset" your constellation of dots? What new opportunities for service have appeared as a result of this difficulty? How, in this experience, might you see your ego diminish so that your relationship with God grows? Write several sentences about how you can respond during your crisis in order to live out your life of significance.

1. _____

2. _____

3. _____

4. _____

5. _____

6. _____

Jean-Pierre de Caussade, in his classic treatise, *Self-Abandonment to Divine Providence*, urges us to practice saying "I will" in response to everything God asks of us. As an example, Caussade uses the two thieves who were crucified alongside Christ. One chose to use his last moments to taunt Jesus. The other chose to transcend his condition and trust that Jesus would take care of him, saying, "Jesus, remember me when You come into Your kingdom."[8] We, in our moments of pain, have a similar choice. We can be filled with self-pity, resenting those closest to us. Or we can do what Caussade suggests and say "I will" to every challenge that comes our way: I will submit to God's will. I will accept the challenge ahead. I will love and serve those around me. I will choose not to blame God or others. I will see this challenge as an opportunity to reconnect with my ultimate purpose in life. I will be fully present today. In the process of responding, "I will," we experience the blessing of "the peace of God, which surpasses all understanding" (Philippians 4:7), a phrase that Reverend Gerald B. Kieschnick likes to say, "means just that."[9]

Walter Ciszek, an American Jesuit priest serving in Eastern Poland, was arrested by the Soviets during World War II, accused of being a spy. Father Ciszek was placed in solitary confinement for five years in Moscow, served fifteen years of hard labor, and another three years of exile in Siberia, before being returned to the United States twenty-three years later. It is hard to imagine the hardship and cruelty of his experience. The priest later acknowledged, however, that his greatest suffering was emotional, when he pitied himself because of the injustice of his fate. Through his experience, Ciszek learned that when he abandoned himself to God, reminding himself that this prison is where God wanted him to be at that particular time, he felt an immense feeling of freedom and peace, "a feeling of joy, that confidence in the simple and direct faith expressed in trusting [God] alone."[10]

Father Ciszek discovered that it was possible to live a life of significance even in a Soviet prison camp. He discovered and lived a life of service to his fellow prisoners, serving as Christ's representative in a place of little hope.

As Christians, we respond to our suffering by placing ourselves at the foot of the cross. We may also place ourselves alongside Jesus, and plead, "My Father, if it be possible, let this cup pass from Me; nevertheless, not as I will, but as You will" (Matthew 26:39). We pray with the assurance that even though God may not take away our suffering, He will bless us through it.

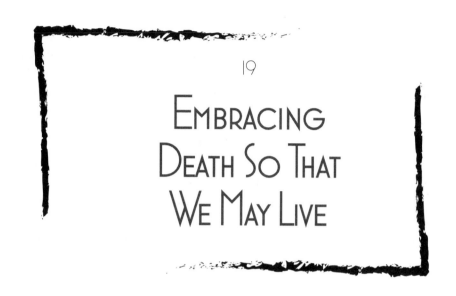

19

Embracing Death So That We May Live

Come now, you who say, "Today or tomorrow we will go into such and such a town and spend a year there and trade and make a profit"— yet you do not know what tomorrow will bring. What is your life? For you are a mist that appears for a little time and then vanishes. Instead you ought to say, "If the Lord wills, we will live and do this or that."

—James 4:13–15

We live in a society that equates death with failure. Except in those circumstances that involve those close to us, we generally avoid the topic. The idea of *embracing* death, therefore, seems strange—even macabre. Western culture comes from the perspective that if you can't *cure* that which leads to death, it's best to ignore it. But death is a reality that is here to stay. And along with death comes fear surrounding the unspeakable horror of what will be the absence of our existence. The younger we are, the further away death seems. Our focus early on is on gaining education, finding a career, establishing a family, and other pursuits that, by the world's standards, help secure our status as indestructible, if not immortal! However, these distractions are merely a cover up, an illusion that refuses to go away.

Theories and philosophies about death and dying abound. The Bible, however, tells us that death is the result of sin. "For the wages of sin is death, but the free gift of God is eternal life in Christ Jesus our Lord" (Romans 6:23). For believers in Christ, death is not the end of the story; it is the beginning of life. This is what makes the Good News of the Gospel really good! As Martin Luther says, "Jesus' death is the death of death."[1] We still must die. But because of Jesus' death and resurrection, death has lost its hold on us. "O death, where is your victory? O death, where is your sting?" (1 Corinthians 15:55). The reality of our resurrection is reflected throughout the history of the Church, as believers, by their Baptism, make public pronouncements that they are "dying" to the earthly world. This washing is not merely symbolic, but is the actual washing away of the sin that condemns, and the rising again with Christ. In the Early Church, this sacrament was considered extremely subversive in the existing culture. Unfortunately, the subversive nature of our Christian faith has, to a large degree, been lost today. We need reminding that, especially in the postmodern world, we are called to daily discipleship in which we die to the ways of the world in order that we might live for God.

Death isn't the final word, for we pass through death to eternal life. Based on that assurance, we can embrace death and, thereby, truly live for today. Our Christian faith frees us from seeing death as the final exclamation point. Because we don't know when our death will come, every day is an occasion to retrace our steps to see where our life has led us to this point. And we can awake every day to shape a new life of significance. In viewing life from the perspective of our death, we see that *how* we live is what matters, not what we do. So, when we embrace death with hope, we are freed to live life fully. We comprehend the meaning of Jesus' words, "Whoever finds his life will lose it, and whoever loses his life for My sake will find it" (Matthew 10:39).

"Vanity of vanities! All is vanity," speaks the Preacher in Ecclesiastes. "What does man gain by all the toil at which he toils under the sun? A generation goes, and a generation comes, but the earth remains forever. . . . There is no remembrance of former things, nor will there be any remembrance of later things yet to be among those who come after" (Ecclesiastes 1:2–4, 11). Understanding both the futility and the eternal significance of our lives, we view our vocational landscape differently. We are able to discern what is and isn't important. We can allow our own ego to fade as we grow in service toward others. And we come to understand that status and earthly possessions pale in the light of our acts of compassion. Grafted into Christ by the ultimate symbol of death—the cross—we make decisions that please God and benefit others. We bear fruit that lasts.

Imagine yourself at age 70, 80, or even 100. Think about how you might review your life, and ask yourself, "Who have I served? How have I responded to God's call for me to live with significance in every area of my life?" I have offered thoughts and suggestions intended to help us answer these questions as they apply to the four primary vocations of life—family, profession, community, and church. My hope is that you have seen how, by our daily habits formed by compassionate service, we carve a path that enables you to answer these questions above with a sense of satisfaction and peace. When we focus on *how* we live out our discipleship, *what* we do with our life will take care of itself.

> When we focus on how we live out
> our discipleship, what we do with
> our life will take care of itself.

I don't mean to suggest that by living today with the end in mind we know exactly what our plan of action is to get from "here" to "there." Rather, embracing the reality of our death allows us to examine all our actions through the lens of our Christian faith. Is our life filled with significance, or does it lack meaning? Are we truly serving God by our actions, or have we replaced God with idols? Certainly, we are tempted daily to follow the ways of the world. But we live in forgiveness. The Holy Spirit works good even out of our mistakes and bad choices, so that they become stepping stones along the path of our discipleship.

The Strategies

When we keep our death ever before us, we can assess our life accurately. If the fear of death constantly nags at us, it may be that we have lost sight of God's promises and have instead considered our possessions and status as significant. When God is at the center of our hearts, however, our priorities fall into place. When we avail ourselves of the Means of Grace in worship and sharing of the Word, when we forego our ego and live instead for Christ, we can embrace our death. In other words, as Christians, we can "use" the prospect of our death for a life on earth that benefits others.

Viewing life along the two curves is an especially helpful exercise as we think about our own death. We must be ready to die today if we are to be prepared to die in the future. From the present-curve perspective, we ask whether, if we were to die tomorrow, we would be at peace knowing how our actions have served others. We need not be afraid to ask how we might have done things differently. Henri Nouwen, writing in his journal toward the end of his life, describes how to live each day in the face of our eventual death:

> How much longer will I live? . . . Only one thing seems clear to me. Every day should be well lived. What a simple truth! Still, it is worth my attention. Did I offer peace today? Did I bring a smile to someone's face? Did I say words of healing? Did I let go of my anger and resentments? Did I forgive? Did I love? Those are the real questions! I must trust that the little bit of love that I sow now will bear many fruits, here in this world and in the life to come.[2]

In reviewing our lives, we consider if our affairs are in order, and whether we have done all we can to ensure our families will be cared for. We determine if we put a succession plan at work, and if we have practiced responsible stewardship in assigning our resources. We look inward to see if we are prepared to face any suffering that we might endure during our dying and death. We ask, "Am I living my life in a manner so that death does not find me unprepared?" The odds are that you and I will be alive tomorrow. Our calling is to live as if we won't be.

In the midst of living fully for today, we must also prepare to live a life of significance for the future. For this, as mentioned earlier, we must look both ways—back at our life up to this point and ahead to anticipate what awaits us, to the degree we can do so. I begin this exercise by imagining that several decades have come and gone, and I am now 90 years old. What do I see? How do I feel? I am secure in the knowledge that all my sins are forgiven. I envision having my family and friends at my side. We share the memories we have made, and I am joyful at the legacy I will leave of wearing God's masks to serve others. I recall fondly how God has used me to serve individuals and organizations. I look forward to the glory that awaits me and to the joyful reunion with all believers on the Day of Resurrection. Looking backward from that vantage point, I now assess what I need to do today, at age 50, and for the next forty years as I move toward the goals I envision. What rituals—as a father, husband, and employer—do I need to establish to help make my hoped-for future a reality? Knowing that, along the horizon of eternity, I am on this earth for a brief moment, I redouble my efforts to live a life worthy of Christ's calling to serve Him and others, whether I die tomorrow or at 90.

> The odds are that you and I will be alive tomorrow. Our calling is to live as if we won't be.

How we die is not only the last witness we leave our loved ones—it likely will also have the greatest impact. We can *die well*, secure in the knowledge that our Lord Jesus Christ lives! As humans, we fear the prospect of death, yet hope that our entire life, up until our last moment on this earth, we have served as a witness and role model. We pray that God might use the example of how we lived to help prepare our loved ones to die well. Consider the example of Cardinal Joseph Bernardin, who served for years as the widely respected and revered archbishop of Chicago. At a press conference in which it was announced that he had terminal cancer, Cardinal Bernardin used the occasion to share that he planned to use his remaining months to strengthen his relationship with God while continuing to serve those around him. He ended by acknowledging that the greatest gift he can continue to give is how he prepares for death and to allow others to share in the experience.[3]

Scripture says "the last enemy to be destroyed is death" (1 Corinthians 15:26). But, when the time comes, we welcome death as the door through which we pass to eternal life. It is the end of our ego and of earthly attachments. As the apostle Paul reminds us, "we brought nothing into the world, and we cannot take anything out of the world" (1 Timothy 6:7). By virtue of our Baptism, we are able to say with Paul, we "die every day!" (1 Corinthians 15:31). And, by the power of the Holy Spirit, we rise daily to a new life of significance—a life marked by the deep meaning of compassionate service, as we follow in the footsteps of the One who came to serve. Only by embracing our death fully are we free to pursue our calling in this life fully.

By the power of the Holy Spirit, we rise daily to a new life of significance—a life marked by the deep meaning of compassionate service, as we follow in the footsteps of the One who came to serve.

Therefore, when we, as Christians, talk about a funeral as a cause for celebration, we are not denying the tremendous grief and sadness that accompany death. The cause for celebration is that the suffering of one of God's own has ended, and he or she now lives on in glory. For that reason, we can say,

"I have fought the good fight, I have finished the race, I have kept the faith. Henceforth there is laid up for me the crown of righteousness" (2 Timothy 4:7–8). In joy, we accept our call to die every day as we patiently wait to receive the inheritance of eternal life that has been prepared for us.

PART FOUR

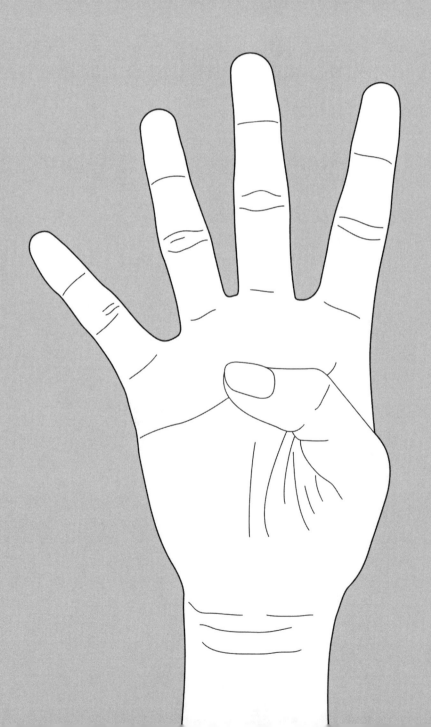

LIVE A LIFE
OF SIGNIFICANCE

The life that intends to be wholly obedient, wholly submissive, wholly listening, is astonishing in its completeness. Its joys are ravishing, its peace profound, its humility the deepest, its power world shaking, its love enveloping, its simplicity that of a trusting child.
—Thomas Kelly[1]

The young prince in Samuel Johnson's classic novel *The History of Rasselas, Prince of Abissinia*, laments, "We desire, we pursue, we obtain, we are satiated; we desire something else and begin a new pursuit."[2] He reaches this conclusion after discovering it is impossible to obtain happiness in this world. The prince pursued that which we all strive for, but which has been given us in our Baptism. We need not be consumed with anxiety at the prospect of our eventual death. This assurance of life eternal enables us to live our temporal lives with meaning, pursue our unique callings from God, and use the gifts of God in our worship and work. In response to the prince's lament, the princess says, "To me, the choice of life is become less important; I hope hereafter to think only on the choice of eternity."[3] We can embrace her conclusion.

To live a life of significance is a daily public witness of our Baptism.

Where we could not, because of our sin, have chosen to follow Christ, the Holy Spirit, working through our Baptism, ushers us into the life of faith and of discipleship. As a result, we can choose the life of significance to which Jesus calls us. We can obediently respond, "I will," to that whichHe demands of us. Dietrich Bonhoeffer says it plainly, "only he who believes is obedient, and only he who is obedient believes."[4] In essence, to live a life of significance is a daily public witness of our Baptism. We encounter God as we serve our family, profession, community, and church. Our faith and our calling are a meld of our hearts, where Christ dwells, and our actions, by which we make Christ known. When God calls us, we have no choice but to follow and do His will.

20

ACCEPTING GOD'S CALL

Fear not, for I have redeemed you;
I have called you by name, you are Mine.
—Isaiah 43:1

t is an understatement to say that living a Christ-filled life in a postmodern world that preaches that life is value-free, and that there is nothing beyond death, is a challenge. We know how the story ends. The final chapter has been written. We live for Christ here and now, and we die only to see Him face-to-face. It is like reading the last chapter of a great mystery first. We take up Paul's plea, "I therefore, a prisoner for the Lord, urge you to walk in a manner worthy of the calling to which you have been called, with all humility and gentleness, with patience, bearing with one another in love, eager to maintain the unity of the Spirit in the bond of peace" (Ephesians 4:1–3). Life in Christ transforms us. As He called the first disciples, Christ calls us to a radically new existence. We are bold in our prayers and actions. By faith we grasp that God "is able [and willing] to do far more abundantly than all that we ask or think" (Ephesians 3:20). We can live boldly as we, with integrity, pursue a life that is truly countercultural.

Because of the magnitude of God's call, there will be times we scramble to escape—like Moses hiding behind his slowness of speech, or Jonah cowering in a ship's hold. But we scramble instead to the cross. Forgiven and restored, the Spirit empowers us to do that which seems impossible, "Truly, truly I say to you, whoever believes in Me will also do the works that I do; and greater works than these will he do, because I am going to the Father. Whatever you ask in My name, this I will do, that the Father may be glorified in the Son. If you ask Me anything in My name, I will do it" (John 14:12–14). Think about it—Jesus healed the sick, fed the multitudes, gave sight to the blind, made the lame to walk. Will we do greater things? Yes, and all because we believe in Jesus will we do the works Jesus does. Whatever we ask in His name He will do to the glory of the Father. The possibilities are endless; the responsibility immense.

Living out our calling is not for the faint of heart. It may require us to take a path that parents, friends, or spouse do not completely understand. It may require us to speak the truth that could result in personal sacrifice. Others may ridicule us for decisions that seem out of touch with the world's reality. Following our call will on occasion bring us to our knees in exhaustion. No, this is not easy work. But it is worthwhile, for we will one day rest, knowing that we have made the most of our gifts in striving to fulfill the biblical charge, "Whatever your hand finds to do, do it with your might" (Ecclesiastes 9:10). Our day-to-day service becomes easier when we walk about (Greek: *peripateo*) wet with the water of our Baptism (Romans 6:4). Nourished by God's Word, spoken, broken, and poured, our deepest needs are fulfilled. Thus restored, we continue our journey by putting our faith into action through works of service performed with the compassion of Christ. Our intuition, informed and moderated by our faith, guides us in knowing which of our activities to embrace and which to let go; whom to spend time with and whom to avoid; when to speak boldly and when to remain silent; how to live and how to die. In so doing, we realize that our worship and our work are mirror images. We discover that we are living lives of significance.

Living in Austin, Texas, I have occasion to attend a University of Texas football game along with about 100,000 other diehard fans. I like to imagine that the deafening roar of the crowd at the sight of the Longhorns taking the field is something like the cheers of encouragement of the generations of saints who have gone before us. "Therefore, since we are surrounded by so great a cloud of witnesses, let us lay aside every weight, and sin which cling so closely, and let us run with endurance the race that is before us" (Hebrews 12:1). These saints—Christians of every culture and race and time—encourage me at every turn. "Forgetting what lies behind and straining forward to what lies ahead, I press on toward the goal for the prize of the upward call of God in Christ Jesus" (Philippians 3:13–15). This, to me, is what it means to live a *life of significance*.

How to Use This Book

f you believe as strongly as we do in the message of this book, you may already be thinking about how to share it with others as part of living your life of significance. Here are some ideas that might be helpful.

Give the book to family, friends, colleagues, and even strangers as a gift. They not only receive a wonderful gift, they also will experience a glimpse of how you shine your light.

If you have a Web site or blog, consider sharing the message of this book with others and how it impacted your life. Recommend they read it as well and link them to **www.cph.org** and **www.kurtsenske.com**. Share the news with your friends on Facebook and other social media Web sites.

Write a book review for your church newsletter, local paper, favorite magazine, or Web site. Recommend to your pastor that your congregation utilize this book in its adult and youth Sunday School classes, and women's and men's Bible studies. Ask your local Christian radio station to have you or the author on as a guest. To contact the author, go to **www.kurtsenske.com**.

Consider putting the book on display in your office, store, or business. To order additional copies, visit **www.cph.org**. To receive a volume discount, call Concordia toll-free at **1-800-325-3040**. A portion of the proceeds will go to benefit Lutheran Social Services. Buy a set of books for your church library, small group participants, children's treatment center, local Christian high school, retirement community, prisons, and the like where people might be influenced by its message.

Talk to others in person, via e-mail lists, or forums that you frequent, sharing how this book has had an impact on your life.

Collectively, we can let our lights shine as we care for God's earth and His people.

ENDNOTES

CHAPTER ONE

1. Dietrich Bonhoeffer, *Discipleship* (Minneapolis: Fortress Press, 2001), 61–62.

CHAPTER THREE

1. Gene Edward Vieth, Jr., *The Spirituality of the Cross*, rev. ed. (St. Louis: Concordia, 2010), 103.

2. Robert Benne, *Ordinary Saints: An Introduction to the Christian Life* (Minneapolis: Fortress Press, 2003), 96–97.

3. Quoted in Thomas R. Kelly, *A Testament of Devotion* (New York: Harper & Brothers, 1941), 52.

4. Douglas J. Schuurman, *Vocation: Discerning Our Callings in Life* (Grand Rapids: Eerdmans, 2004), 123–24.

5. Schuurman, *Vocation*, 88.

6. This thought came in part from Uwe Siemon-Netto, "Being Lutheran: Vocation versus the Postmodern 'Oops.' " *The Cresset* 71.1 (Michaelmas 2007): 36.

CHAPTER FIVE

1. Lao-tzu, *The Way of Lao-tzu* (Chinese philosopher, 604–531 BC).

Part Two

1. Viktor E. Frankl, *Man's Search for Ultimate Meaning* (New York: Perseus, 2000), 157.

Chapter Six

1. Howard and Phyllis Rutledge with Mel and Lyla White, *In The Presence of Mine Enemies* (Old Tappan, NJ: Fleming Revell, 1973), 34.

2. Eileen Flynn, "Pastor Goes 60-60 to Build Spiritual Connection," *Austin American Statesman*, December 13, 2008, G4.

3. Thomas R. Kelly, *A Testament of Devotion* (New York: Harper & Brothers, 1941), 114, 116 (emphasis Kelly).

4. Gordon MacDonald, *Ordering Your Private World* (Nashville: Thomas Nelson, 2003), 23–24.

5. Robert Benne, *Ordinary Saints: An Introduction to the Christian Life* (Minneapolis: Fortress Press, 2003), 46.

6. John Burke, *Soul Revolution: How Imperfect People Become All God Intended* (Grand Rapids: Zondervan, 2008), 49–62.

7. MacDonald, *Ordering Your Private World*, 177.

8. MacDonald, *Ordering Your Private World*, 84 (emphasis MacDonald).

9. Richard J. Foster, *Freedom of Simplicity: Finding Harmony in a Complex World* (San Francisco: Harper, 2005), 99.

10. Brother Lawrence, *The Practice of the Presence of God* (Amberson, PA: Scroll Pub., 2007), 24.

Chapter Seven

1. Douglas J. Schuurman, *Vocation: Discerning Our Callings in Life* (Grand Rapids: Eerdmans, 2004), 126.

Chapter Eight

1. Aristotle, *Politics*.

2. Jim Loehr and Tony Schwartz, *The Power of Full Engagement: Managing Energy, Not Time, Is the Key to High Performance and Personal Renewal* (New York: Simon & Schuster, 2003), 13.

3. Loehr and Schwartz, *Power of Full Engagement*, 15–17. See also Kurt Senske, *Personal Values: God's Game Plan for Life* (Minneapolis: Augsburg, 2004), 57–59.

4. For a summary of the medical evidence that supports this claim, see Kurt Senske, *Personal Values: God's Game Plan for Life* (Minneapolis: Augsburg, 2004), 33–52.

5. Thomas Addington and Thomas Graves, "Balance: Life's Juggling Act," *Life@Work* (November–December, 2000): 40, 43.

6. Thomas R. Kelly, *A Testament of Devotion* (New York: Harper & Brothers, 1941), 116.

7. Laura Nash and Howard Stevenson, "Success That Lasts," *Harvard Business Review* (February 2004): 102.

8. Nash and Stevenson, "Success That Lasts," 105.

9. Kelly, *A Testament of Devotion*, 114–15.

Chapter Nine

1. Quoted in Kim Manley, et al, *International Practice Development in Nursing and Healthcare* (West Sussex: Blackwell, 2008), 101.

2. Morton T. Kelsey, "The Cross and the Cellar," *Bread and Wine: Readings for Lent and Easter* (Maryknoll, NY: Orbis Books, 2003), 206, 210–11.

3. Kelsey, "The Cross and the Cellar," 206.

4. Jim Loehr, *The Power of Story: Rewrite Your Destiny in Business and in Life* (New York: Free Press, 2007), 138–39.

5. Loehr, *The Power of Story*, 41–42.

6. Loehr, *The Power of Story*, 89.

7. Loehr, *The Power of Story*, 33.

8. Dietrich Bonhoeffer, *Letters and Papers from Prison*, ed. Eberhard Bethge (New York: Macmillan Co., 1953), 23.

9. Loehr, *The Power of Story*, 167 (emphasis Loehr).

10. Loehr, *The Power of Story*, 201–2.

Chapter Ten

1. Jimmy Carter, *Why Not the Best?* (Nashville, TN: Broadman Press, 1975), Introduction.

2. Carol Dweck, *Mindset: The New Psychology of Success* (New York: Random House, 2006).

3. See Ken Blanchard and Terry Waghorn, *Mission Possible: Becoming a World-Class Organization While There's Still Time* (New York: McGraw Hill, 1997), 17. See also Kurt Senske, *Executive Values: A Christian Approach to Organizational Leadership* (Minneapolis: Augsburg, 2003), 107–8.

4. Geoff Colvin, *Talent Is Overrated: What Really Separates World-Class Performers from Everybody Else* (New York: Portfolio, 2008).

5. Malcolm Gladwell, *Outliers: The Story of Success* (New York: Little, Brown & Co., 2008), 38–40.

6. Gladwell, *Outliers*, 40.

7. Anthony Robbins, *Awakening the Giant Within: How to Take Immediate Control of Your Mental, Emotional, Physical and Financial Destiny* (New York: Free Press, 1991), 43.

Chapter Eleven

1. Victor E. Frankl, *Man's Search for Ultimate Meaning* (New York: Perseus, 2000), Preface.

2. Mihaly Csikszentmihalyi, *Flow: The Psychology of Optimal Experience* (New York: Harper Perennial, 1991), 4.

3. Csikszentmihalyi, *Flow*, 119.

4. Csikszentmihalyi, *Flow*, 169.

5. Csikszentmihalyi, *Flow*, 171.

6. Csikszentmihalyi, *Flow*, 175.

7. Csikszentmihalyi, *Flow*, 213–18.

8. Csikszentmihalyi, *Flow*, 6.

9. Csikszentmihalyi, *Flow*, 209–13.

10. Csikszentmihalyi, *Flow*, 190–91.

11. Eckhart Tolle, *A New Earth: Awakening to Your Life's Purpose* (New York: Penguin Group, 2005), 76.

12. Tolle, *A New Earth*, 79.

Chapter Twelve

1. Montaigne, *Essays*. III. 10.

2. William Placher, ed., *Callings: Twenty Centuries of Christian Wisdom on Vocation* (Grand Rapids: Eerdmans, 2005), 9.

3. Eckhart Tolle, *A New Earth: Awakening to Your Life's Purpose* (New York: Penguin Group, 2005), 35.

4. Tolle, *A New Earth*, 36–37.

5. Deion Sanders, "The Game of Football Can't Love You Back," *Austin American Statesman* (November 11, 2006): B2.

6. Tolle, *A New Earth*, 40.

7. Robert Frank, "How the Rich Spend Their Time: Stressed," *The Wall Street Journal*, June 4, 2008.

8. Frank, "How the Rich Spend Their Time."

9. Mihaly Csikszentmihalyi, *Flow: The Psychology of Optimal Experience* (Harper Perennial: New York, 1991), 19.

10. Quoted in Robert Ellsberg, *The Saints' Guide to Happiness* (New York: North Point Press, 2003), 14.

11. Barbara Cawthorne Crafton, "Living Lent," in *Bread and Wine: Readings for Lent and Easter* (Maryknoll, NY: Orbis, 2005), 15, 18.

12. Csikszentmihalyi, *Flow*, 13.

13. Rochelle Melander and Harold Eppley, *Our Lives Are Not Our Own* (Minneapolis: Augsburg Fortress, 2005), 73, quoted in Jack Fortin, *The Centered Life* (Minneapolis: Augsburg Fortress, 2006), 79.

14. Tolle, *A New Earth*, 46.

Chapter Thirteen

1. Martin Luther, *The Freedom of the Christian Man*, as quoted in Garth D. Ludwig, *Order Restored: A Biblical Interpretation of Health Medicine and Healing* (St. Louis: Concordia, 1999), 127.

2. For a detailed discussion of the concept of *wholeness* as it relates to the living out of our Christ-based lives, see Kurt Senske, *Personal Values: God's Game Plan for Life* (Minneapolis: Augsburg, 2004).

3. Ludwig, *Order Restored*, 139.

4. Gordon MacDonald, *Ordering Your Private World* (Nashville: Thomas Nelson, 2003), 192–96.

5. MacDonald, *Ordering Your Private World*, 205.

6. Roy M. Oswald, "Foreword," in *The Spiritual Leader's Guide to Self-Care*, Rochelle Melander and Harold Eppley (Bethesda, MD: Alban Institute, 2002), x. See also Kurt Senske, *Personal Values: God's Game Plan for Life* (Minneapolis: Augsburg, 2004), 65.

7. Quoted in Senske, *Personal Values*, 67.

8. Dietrich Bonhoeffer, *The Cost of Discipleship* (New York: Macmillan, 1963), 98.

Part Three

1. *Preface to Paradise Lost* by C. S. Lewis, copyright © C. S. Lewis Pte. Ltd. 1942.

Chapter Fourteen

1. Robert Bellah, et al, *The Good Society* (New York: Knopf, 1991), 48.

2. Kurt Senske, *Executive Values: A Christian Approach to Organizational Leadership* (Minneapolis: Augsburg, 2003), 135.

3. The Lutheran Church—Missouri Synod Health Ministries and Department of Human Resources, *Executive Health* (February 2001). See also Senske, *Executive Values*, 135–36.

4. Senske, *Executive Values*, 140–41.

5. See Kurt Senske, *Personal Values: God's Game Plan for Life* (Minneapolis: Augsburg, 2004), 33–52, 72–89.

6. Douglas J. Schuurman, *Vocation: Discerning Our Callings in Life* (Grand Rapids: Eerdmans, 2004), 124.

7. Schuurman, *Vocation*, 163.

8. Some of these thoughts came from Eckhart Tolle, *A New Earth: Awakening to Your Life's Purpose* (New York: Penguin Group, 2005), 104–6.

9. Naomi Schafer Riley, "Defend the Orphan: An Age-Old Christian Lesson Gets a New Lease on Life," *Wall Street Journal*, August 29, 2008, W9.

10. William Placher, ed., *Callings: Twenty Centuries of Christian Wisdom on Vocation* (Eerdmans: Grand Rapids, 2005), 9.

11. Schuurman, *Vocation*, 175.

12. Sue Shellenbarger, "On the Virtues of Making Your Children Do the Dishes," *The Wall Street Journal*, August 27, 2008, D1.

13. Mihaly Csikszentmihalyi, *Flow: The Psychology of Optimal Experience* (New York; Harper Perennial, 1990), 88–89.

14. Csikszentmihalyi, *Flow*, 88.

15. Joseph B. Verrengia, "Compassion at Stake for Families in Motion," *Science and Theology News* (May 2005): 1, 3.

16. Richard Foster, *Freedom of Simplicity: Finding Harmony in a Complex World* (San Francisco: Harper, 2004), 169.

17. Dietrich Bonhoeffer, *Letters and Papers from Prison*, ed. Eberhard Bethge (New York: Macmillan, 1953), 47–48.

CHAPTER FIFTEEN

1. D. Michael Bennethum, *Listen! God Is Calling! Luther Speaks of Vocation, Faith, and Work* (Minneapolis: Augsburg Fortress, 2003), 46.

2. Bennethum, *Listen!*, 51.

3. Michael Kimmelman, *The Accidental Masterpiece: On the Art of Life and Vice Versa* (New York: Penguin Press, 2005), 6.

4. Gordon MacDonald, *Ordering Your Private World* (Nashville: Thomas Nelson, 2003), 29–40, 57–68.

5. From vol. 1 of *Luther's Church Postil: Gospels: Advent, Christmas and Epiphany Sermons*, in *The Precious and Sacred Writings of Martin Luther*, ed. John Nicholas Lenker (Minneapolis: Lutherans in All Lands, 1905), 10:246, quoted in Douglas J. Schuurman, *Vocation: Discerning Our Callings in Life* (Grand Rapids: Eerdmans, 2004), 160.

6. Albert Schweitzer, *Out of My Life and Thought: An Autobiography*, trans. C. T. Campion (New York: Henry Holt and Co., 1949), 91, quoted in Schuurman, *Vocation*, 159–60.

7. Bonnie Miller Rubin and Jeremy Manier, "Our Pursuit of Happiness," *Chicago Tribune*, October 5, 2008, Sec. 1, 1, 18.

8. Mihaly Csikszentmihalyi, *Flow: The Psychology of Optimal Experience* (New York: Harper Perennial, 1990), 213.

9. Roy M. Oswald, "Foreword," *The Spiritual Leader's Guide to Self-Care*, Rochelle Melander and Harold Eppley (Bethesda, MD: Alban Institute 2002), x. For more information on polarities in congregations, see Roy M. Oswald and Barry Johnson, *Managing Polarities in Congregations: Eight Keys for Thriving Faith Communities* (Herndon, VA: Alban Institute, 2010).

10. Gene Edward Veith, Jr., *The Spirituality of the Cross*, rev. ed. (St. Louis: Concordia, 2010), 114. See also pp. 112–14.

11. Bennethum, *Listen!*, 63–64.

12. Eckhart Tolle, *A New Earth: Awakening to Your Life's Purpose* (New York: Penguin Group, 2005), 91.

13. Tolle, *A New Earth*, 93.

14. Tolle, *A New Earth*, 109; see also pp. 121–22.

15. Jack Fortin, *The Centered Life* (Minneapolis: Augsburg Fortress, 2006), 52.

16. Quoted in Bennethum, *Listen!*, 48–49.

Chapter Sixteen

1. Luther, Martin, "The Freedom of the Christian Man," in vol. 31 of *Luther's Works: Career of the Reformer I*, ed. Harold J. Grimm, Luther's Works (Philadelphia: Fortress), 31:371.

2. Martin Luther King Jr., *The Measure of a Man* (Philadelphia: Fortress Press, 1988), 43–44.

3. King Jr., *The Measure of a Man*, 44.

4. Quoted from Reed Lessing, *Mercy in The Old Testament* (LCMS World Relief and Human Care, 2007), 12.

5. Fyodor Dostoevksy, *The Brothers Karamazov*, trans. David Magarshack (New York: Penguin, 1958), 61–63, quoted in Robert Ellsberg, *The Saint's Guide to Happiness* (New York: North Point Press, 2003), 92.

6. Personal conversation with Matthew Harrison, July 21, 2007.

7. Richard Foster, *Freedom of Simplicity: Finding Harmony in a Complex World* (San Francisco: Harper, 2005) 23.

8. Foster, *Freedom of Simplicity*, 22–23. See also Malachi 3:10; Isaiah 1:19.

9. Foster, *Freedom of Simplicity*, 23.

10. Matthew C. Harrison, *Christ Have Mercy: How to Put Your Faith in Action* (St. Louis: Concordia, 2008), 40.

11. For a more thorough discussion of the history and use of the word *splanchnon*, see Harrison, *Christ Have Mercy*, 40–44.

12. Arthur Simon, *How Much Is Enough? Hungering for God in an Affluent Culture* (Grand Rapids: Baker, 2003), 148.

13. An excellent resource is Mark Allan Powell, *Giving to God: The Bible's Good News about Living a Generous Life* (Grand Rapids: Eerdmans, 2006).

14. Mark Allan Powell, "Where You Put Your Treasure . . . That's Where Your Heart Will Go," *The Lutheran* (November 2006): 17.

15. For a summary of the various scientific studies on this topic, see Kurt Senske, *Personal Values: God's Game Plan for Life* (Minneapolis: Augsburg, 2004), 33–51.

16. Tara Parker-Pope, "In Month of Giving, a Healthy Reward," *The Wall Street Journal*, December 1, 2009, D5.

17. Parker-Pope, "In Month of Giving."

18. Parker-Pope, "In Month of Giving." See also Cami Walker, *29 Gifts: How a Month of Giving Can Change Your Life* (Cambridge, MA: Da Capo Press, 2009).

Chapter Seventeen

1. Donald Heiges, *The Christian Calling* (Philadelphia: Fortress Press, 1958), 41, quoted in Douglas J. Schuurman, *Vocation: Discerning Our Callings in Life* (Grand Rapids: Eerdmans, 2004), 35.

2. Robert Bellah, et al, *The Good Society* (New York: Knopf, 1991), 183.

3. Tom Sine, "Small Wonders," *Christianity Today*, www.christianitytoday.com/le/currenttrendscolumns/culturewatch/18.15.html?start=1.

4. Schuurman, *Vocation*, 18.

5. Gary Gunderson with Larry Pray, *Leading Causes of Life* (Memphis: The Center of Excellence in Faith and Health, Methodist LeBonheur Healthcare, 2006), 51.

6. Gunderson and Pray, *Leading Causes of Life*, 71.

CHAPTER EIGHTEEN

1. Lutheran Social Services Staff Devotion, October 28, 2008, Austin, Texas.

2. Bradley Hanson, *A Graceful Life: Lutheran Spirituality for Today* (Minneapolis: Augsburg, 2000), 69.

3. Matthew Harrison, "Though God Slay Me, I Will Yet Hope in Him," *Mercy Works* (Fall 2006/Winter 2007): 4, 7, fn. 6.

4. Matthew Harrison, "Though God Slay Me, I Will Yet Hope in Him," *Mercy Works* (Fall 2006/Winter 2007): 4, 7, fn. 4.

5. Douglas J. Schuurman, *Vocation: Discerning Our Callings in Life* (Grand Rapids: Eerdmans, 2004), 149.

6. Some of these thoughts came from Eckhart Tolle, *A New Earth: Awakening to Your Life's Purpose* (New York: Penguin, 2006), 101–3.

7. Michael Weisskopf, "My Right Hand," *Time Magazine* (October 2, 2006): 27.

8. Robert Ellsberg, *The Saints' Guide to Happiness* (New York: North Point Press, 2003), 120–21. Cf. Luke 23:42.

9. Texas District Convention, The Lutheran Church—Missouri Synod, Speech to Delegates, June 26, 2009.

10. Fr. Walter J. Ciszek, S.J. with Fr. Daniel Flaherty, S.J., *He Leadeth Me* (San Francisco: Ignatius Press, 1995), 30.

Chapter Nineteen

1. Bryan Wolfmueller, "Consolation at the End of Life in Luther's Theology," *Mercy Works* 1, no. 3/4 (Fall 2006/Winter 2007): 22, 23.

2. Quoted in Robert Ellsberg, *The Saints' Guide to Happiness* (New York: North Point Press, 2003), 146–47.

3. Joseph Cardinal Bernardin, *The Gift of Peace* (Chicago: Loyola Press, 1997), 134–37.

Part Four

1. Thomas R. Kelly, *A Testament of Devotion* (New York: Harper & Brothers, 1941), 54.

2. Samuel Johnson, *The History of Rasselas, Prince of Abissinia* (Oxford University Press, 1968), 41.

3. Johnson, *Rasselas*, 122.

4. Dietrich Bonhoeffer, *The Call of Discipleship* (New York: Simon & Schuster, 1995), 63.